Spiritual, Life and Values Education for Children

This book offers various perspectives on children's spirituality and its relation to life and values education from diverse socio-cultural and educational contexts. It brings together a collection of select research articles that were published over a period of two decades (1999–2020) in the *International Journal of Children's Spirituality (IJCS)* to celebrate the journal's 25th anniversary.

Featuring contributions by leading international scholars from the U.K., the U.S.A., Canada, Hong Kong, China, and Australia, this volume offers a multidisciplinary snapshot of children's spirituality and its relation to life and values education. It highlights the importance of socio-cultural and religious traditions, as well as perspectives on religious education and the spirituality of children shaped by religious, cultural, and educational systems in specific societies and contexts. Chapters cover topics including the links between mirror neurons and human empathy and education; the relationship between spirituality and citizenship; the notion of inclusive spiritual education and the perspectives of spiritual education through the conceptual lens of transcendence, raised awareness, and spiritualism; how outdoor play spaces can contribute to a child's spiritual development through enriching activities; and approaches to help nurture students' spiritual growth in their aspects of themselves (self), others, the environment, and with a Transcendent Other (transcendence).

This volume will be a key resource for researchers and postgraduate students interested in understanding children's spirituality and its implications for spiritual, life, and values education.

John Chi-Kin Lee is Chair Professor of Curriculum and Instruction, Director of the Centre for Religious and Spirituality Education, and Director of the Academy of Educational Development and Innovation at the Education University of Hong Kong (EdUHK), Hong Kong. He has served as Changjiang Scholar Chair Professor conferred by the Ministry of Education, the People's Republic of China. Professor Lee is also UNESCO Chair in Regional Education Development and Lifelong Learning at the EdUHK and the Southeast Asian Ministers of Education Organization Research Fellow. He has served as the editor of the *International Journal of Children's Spirituality*, executive editor of *Teaching and Teacher Education*, and editorial board member or advisory editor of many local, regional, and international journals. He is also a prolific writer who has edited and written more than 25 books and published over 100 journal articles and book chapters.

Spiritual, Life and Values Education for Children

Edited by
John Chi-Kin Lee

Routledge
Taylor & Francis Group
LONDON AND NEW YORK

First published 2025
by Routledge
4 Park Square, Milton Park, Abingdon, Oxon, OX14 4RN

and by Routledge
605 Third Avenue, New York, NY 10158

Routledge is an imprint of the Taylor & Francis Group, an informa business

British Library Cataloguing-in-Publication Data
A catalogue record for this book is available from the British Library

ISBN13: 978-1-032-61907-1 (hbk)
ISBN13: 978-1-032-61908-8 (pbk)
ISBN13: 978-1-032-61909-5 (ebk)

DOI: 10.4324/9781032619095

Typeset in Myriad Pro
by codeMantra

Publisher's Note
The publisher accepts responsibility for any inconsistencies that may have arisen during the conversion of this book from journal articles to book chapters, namely the inclusion of journal terminology.

Contents

Citation Information

The following chapters were originally published in various volumes and issues of the *International Journal of Children's Spirituality*. When citing this material, please use the original page numbering for each article, as follows:

Introduction (1 of 2)
Children's spirituality, life and values education: cultural, spiritual and educational perspectives
John Chi-Kin Lee
International Journal of Children's Spirituality, volume 25, issue 1 (2020), pp. 1–8

Introduction (2 of 2)
Children's spirituality, life and religious education: socio-cultural and religious traditions and perspectives
John Chi-Kin Lee
International Journal of Children's Spirituality, volume 25, issue 2 (2020), pp. 83–90

Chapter 1
Preparing Spirituality for Citizenship
Jacqueline Watson
International Journal of Children's Spirituality, volume 8, issue 1 (2003), pp. 9–24

Chapter 2
Helps to Fostering Students' Spiritual Health [1]
John W. Fisher
International Journal of Children's Spirituality, volume 4, issue 1 (1999), pp. 29–49

Chapter 3
Attentiveness for children: proposing a neo-confucian curriculum for preschool education
Sandra Wu and Charlene Tan
International Journal of Children's Spirituality, volume 25, issue 2 (2020), pp. 124–140

Chapter 4
A conceptual investigation into the possibility of spiritual education
Ping Ho Wong
International Journal of Children's Spirituality, volume 11, issue 1 (2006), pp. 73–85

Chapter 5

The empathetic mind: the essence of human spirituality
Marian de Souza
International Journal of Children's Spirituality, volume 19, issue 1 (2014), pp. 45–54

Chapter 6

Let's play at the park! Family pathways promoting spiritual resources to inspire nature, pretend play, storytelling, intergenerational play and celebrations
Kathleen I. Harris
International Journal of Children's Spirituality, volume 21, issue 2 (2016), pp. 90–103

Chapter 7

Children's spirituality and theologising with children: the role of 'context'
Annemie Dillen
International Journal of Children's Spirituality, volume 25, issue 3–4 (2020), pp. 238–253

Chapter 8

An inclusive spiritual education
Joyce E. Bellous
International Journal of Children's Spirituality, volume 24, issue 4 (2019), pp. 389–400

Notes on Contributors

Joyce E. Bellous, Christian Faith Education, Taylor Seminary, Edmonton, Canada.

Marian de Souza, School of Religious Education, Australian Catholic University, Ballarat, Australia.

Annemie Dillen, Faculty of Theology and Religious Studies, KU Leuven, Belgium.

John W. Fisher, Federation University Australia, Ballarat, Australia.

Kathleen I. Harris, School of Education and Applied Social Sciences, Seton Hill University, Greensburg, USA.

John Chi-Kin Lee, Centre for Religious and Spirituality Education; Academy of Educational Development and Innovation, The Education University of Hong Kong (EdUHK), Hong Kong.

Charlene Tan, Faculty of Education, The University of Hong Kong, Hong Kong.

Jacqueline Watson, School of Education, University of Exeter, UK.

Ping Ho Wong, Department of International Education and Lifelong Learning, The Hong Kong Institute of Education, Hong Kong.

Sandra Wu, National Institute of Education, Nanyang Technological University, Singapore.

Preface

John Chi-Kin Lee
The Education University of Hong Kong

The preparation of this book is first based on my email communication with Ms Shreya Bajpai Commissioning Editor which is related to Routledge Special-Issue-as-Book (SPIB) published by Taylor & Francis around March 2023. As the editor of the *International Journal of Children's Spirituality* (*IJCS*) from 2020, I have inquired about the feasibility of compiling a collection of published articles and editorials for the journal. Many thanks to Shreya's support and here comes the first book of selected papers and editorials of *IJCS*.

The intention of compiling and editing this book is of twofolds: First is to celebrate the publication of *IJCS* dated back to 1996 and as a tribute to former editors, editorial board members, and contributors for their invaluable contribution; second, the selection of articles and editorials provide a brief and snapshot of selected area(s) of children's spirituality and its relation to values education which may widely encompass diversified types ranging from various traditions of religious education, spiritual education, and life education (Lee, Yip & Kong, 2021) to sex education (e.g., Wilson, 2001), environmental education (e.g., Watson, 2003, p.16), and moral and citizenship education. We live, learn, and work in a world possibly filled with paradoxes and conflicts as well opportunities and prospects. One of these conflicts, as John Hull (1996, p.3) remarked, is that spirituality might be inhibited to some extent by economic socialization and market culture and therefore "a society dedicated to the values of money nevertheless expects its schools to promote the values of human spirituality".

In this book, the two editorials prepared by Lee (2020a, p.1; 2020b, p.83) serve to provide a multidisciplinary and diversified introduction to highlight children's spirituality, life, and values education. This book also discusses the importance of socio-cultural and religious traditions as well as perspectives shaped by religious and cultural and educational systems in specific societies and contexts on life and religious education and spirituality of children.

The paper by Jacqueline Watson (2003) drawing on some literature of *IJCS* attempts to situate elements of spiritual development in the school curriculum which is primarily related to Religious Education in the context of the U.K. There are also other views in the context of Britain that religious education and citizenship education should work together (Erricker, 2003, p.213). Watson (2004, p.267) remarks that citizenship education tends to highlight one-nation values, while religious education inclines to promote diversity and dialogue. However, Watson (2003) highlights the application of spiritual development to personal growth and moral development, which to some extent extends to and resonates the aims of citizenship education (pp.16, 22). John W. Fisher's (1999) empirical study seeks to establish a definition of spiritual health in the context of school curriculum. This definition comprises four relationships that a person has with themselves, others, the environment, and the Transcendent Other (p.30), which correspond to four domains of spiritual well-being: personal, communal, environmental, and global (pp.32, 47–48).

In the diversified Asian contexts, Wu and Tan (2020) propose a neo-Confucian curriculum for preschool education highlighting attentiveness (*Jing*) and emphasizing the need of "nurture… to complement nature" (p.127) and to "bring out the innate goodness and imbue moral values" (p.133). Wong Ping-ho (2006) explores three important aspects of spirituality with different degrees and shads (p.74) which include "transcendence, raised awareness and spiritualism" (p.73). He believes that effective spiritual education is linked with social ethos (p.78) and suggests the possibility of the "emergence model" (p.82) for virtue, language, and spiritual development. Based on the research on mirror neurons, de Souza (2014) advocates the importance of cultivating empathy. There are many insightful approaches such as developing inclusive communities, welcoming and celebrating diversity, appreciating the role of the arts in the development of individual and communal empathy, and valuing the plurality and diversity among students (pp.52–53).

Play at the stage of early childhood education has been identified as an important strategy or approach for nurturing children's spirituality (Mata-McMahon, 2019). The paper by Kathleen I. Harris (2016), drawing on Miller (2015) and others' ideas, highlights that nature and outdoor spaces such as community parks are conducive to spiritual enrichment and awareness (pp.91, 93). She also emphasizes for children's spirituality and family components such as belonging, respect, and appreciation (p.92).

Andrew Wright (1997) suggests that a genuine spiritual education requires a contextualization within a diversity of spiritual traditions (p. 8), which are to some extent associated with national identity and specific religious communities (p.16). Wright (2000) also identifies the possibility of a "process-oriented spiritual pedagogy" (pp.100–101) where spiritual education could become an "ongoing journey of exploration" and alternative views of spiritual traditions could be openly exchanged. Moreover, teaching controversial issues might be applied to spirituality (Wright, 2000, pp.135–136).

Spiritual, life, and values education is understood and enacted by individual, institutions, and educational systems under complicated and plural contexts. Dillen (2020, p.250) suggests that it is important to give more attention to researching "particular experiences of a group of children (illness, migration, death of a father, killed in traumatic circumstances)" and reflexivity about their own contexts (p.251). This might lead to the possible implications that parents, teachers, researchers, peers, and children could collectively reflect and act together to co-construct their preferred approach to spiritual education and nature of children's spirituality. The paper by Joyce Bellous (2019, p.389) proposes an inclusive spiritual education approach and a holistic and humane literacy curriculum that takes into account four types of spiritual styles and embraces "word, emotion, symbol and action".

The limitation of space for this collection as required by Taylor & Francis has made the selection of papers and editorials a difficult task, and there are far more papers from *IJCS* which should have been included in this book if more pages are allowed. Hopefully, these selected papers, while some views could be diverse and contesting with one another, could give readers some inspiring thoughts on children's spirituality and their contexts and connections with spiritual, life, and values education.

Acknowledgment

The authors would like to thank Ms Wendy Hoi Yi Liu for her assistance in preparing this chapter.

Disclosure statement

The views reflected in this article are personal views only and do not represent those of The Education University of Hong Kong and/or the UNESCO, and do not commit these respective organizations.

References

Bellous, J.E. (2019). An inclusive spiritual education. *International Journal of Children's Spirituality*, 24(4), 389–400.

de Souza, M. (2014). The empathetic mind: the essence of human spirituality. *International Journal of Children's Spirituality*, 19(1), 45–54.

Dillen, A. (2020). Children's spirituality and theologizing with children: the role of 'context'. *International Journal of Children's Spirituality*, 25(3-4), 238–253.

Erricker, J. (2003). Editorial: Spiritual citizenship. *International Journal of Children's Spirituality*, 8(3), 211–214.

Fisher, J.W. (1999). Helps to fostering students' spiritual health [1]. *International Journal of Children's Spirituality*, 4(1), 29–49.

Harris, K.I. (2016). Let's play at the park! Family pathways promoting spiritual resources to inspire nature, pretend play, storytelling, intergenerational play and celebrations. *International Journal of Children's Spirituality*, 21(2), 90–103.

Hull, J. (1996). Foreword by Professor John Hull. *International Journal of Children's Spirituality*, 1(1), 3.

Lee, J.C.K. (2020a). Editorial: Children's spirituality, life and values education: cultural, spiritual and educational perspectives. *International Journal of Children's Spirituality*, 25(1), 1–8.

Lee, J.C.K. (2020b). Editorial: children's spirituality, life and religious education: socio-cultural and religious traditions and perspectives. *International Journal of Children's Spirituality*, 25(2), 83–90.

Lee, J.C.K., Yip, S.Y.W. and Kong, R.H.M. (Eds.) (2021). *Life and moral education in Greater China*. London; New York: Routledge.

Mata-McMahon, J. (2019). Finding connections between spirituality and play for early childhood education. *International Journal of Children's Spirituality*, 24(1), 44–57, DOI: 10.1080/1364436X.2019.1619528

Miller, L. (2015). *The spiritual child: the new science on parenting for health and lifelong thriving*. New York: St Martin's Press.

Watson, J. (2003). Preparing spirituality for citizenship. *International Journal of Children's Spirituality*, 8(1), 9–24.

Watson, J. (2004). Educating for citizenship – the emerging relationship between religious education and citizenship education. *British Journal of Religious Education*, 26(3), 259–271.

Wilson, J. (2001). The spiritual and the earthly. *International Journal of Children's Spirituality*, 6(2), 147–157.

Wong, P.H. (2006). A conceptual investigation into the possibility of spiritual education. *International Journal of Children's Spirituality*, 11(1), 73–85.

Wright, A. (1997). Embodied spirituality: the place of culture and tradition in contemporary educational discourse on spirituality. *International Journal of Children's Spirituality*, 1(2), 8–20.

Wright, A. (2000). *Spirituality and education*. London: Routledge/Falmer.

Wu, S. and Tan, C. (2020). Attentiveness for children: proposing a neo-confucian curriculum for preschool curriculum. *International Journal of Children's Spirituality*, 25(2), 124–140.

Introduction (1 of 2)— Children's spirituality, life and values education: cultural, spiritual and educational perspectives

John Chi-Kin Lee

'May the God of hope fill you with all joy and peace in believing, so that by the power of the Holy Spirit you may abound in hope'. (Romans 15:13, English Standard Version)

'Sincerity is the way to heaven. To think how to be sincere is the way of man'. (Mengzi 4A:12)[1]

The International Journal of Children's Spirituality (*IJCS*) being published now is in its 25th volume. Since September 1996, *IJCS* has been one of the leading, multidisciplinary journals related to spirituality, religion and education. Initiated by and indebted to Clive and Jane Erricker and Cathy Ota as well as under the generous auspices of the International Association of Children's Spirituality and with enormous support from past and present editorial board members, readers and reviewers of *IJCS*, I am really honoured to be appointed as the new Editor-in-chief of this important journal indexed by Arts & Humanities Citation Index and other databases and references (https://www.childrenspirituality.org/publications/the-ijcs/; https://www.tandfonline.com/action/journalInformation?journalCode=cijc20).

I would like to express my deep appreciation and gratitude to former Editors Ruth Wills, Adrian Gellel and Karen-Marie Yust for their outstanding contributions with an ambition of making the journal 'to be a voice of a global network that may concretely have a positive impact on the everyday lives of children' (Wills, Gellel, and Yust 2018a, p. 2).

Spirituality is a multidisciplinary field, probably not a discipline, and so its academic and professional inquiry necessitates an interdisciplinary approach with diversified paradigms and methodologies, as well as desirably needs dialogue and collaboration between researchers and practitioners for deepening our holistic understanding and enhancement of spirituality of childhood and young people (Adams, Bull, and Maynes 2016, p. 761; Adams 2017a, p. 1). The spiritual aspect of life is also described as '… helps[helping] individuals create frameworks of meaning and provides[providing] individuals with a way of being in the world which influences their decisions and actions. It enables them to interpret their life experiences …' (Watson 2017, p. 10).

There are various interpretations of spirituality which is closely linked with religion or faith tradition and related to the notion of 'religiosity' (e.g., Eaude 2019; Van der Zee and Tirri 2009, p. 1; Robinson 2017, p. 43 & p. 46; Rossiter 2011, p. 59). However, some consider that religious is not equivalent to spiritual, especially for those who do not have faith identification (Adams, Bull, and Maynes 2016, pp. 761–762; Giesenberg 2007; Robinson 2017, p. 47; Selvam 2013).

Cole (2011, p. 5), based on Love's (2001) and Tisdell's (2003) research in higher education, defines spirituality to reflect 'a child's development of self that includes a search for meaning, transcendence, wholeness, and purpose'. To counteract the traditional cognitive psychology perspective, alternative approaches to understanding the spirituality and spiritual awareness of children which is historically situated and socially constructed covering social, interpersonal and ideological concepts based on post-formalism are promoted (Cole 2011, p. 8; Myers 1997).

While the concept of spirituality tends to be elusive, diverse and sometimes ambiguous, some key themes are frequently found in the literature for spirituality of children (Adams, Bull, and Maynes 2016, p. 768): spirituality as an inherent being; relationality, identity and connectedness (de Souza 2016a, p. 127); creativity; transcendence; spiritual experience; and awe and wonder (Department for Education, Employment and Workplace Relations (DEEWR) 2009, p. 49). The lack of agreed-upon definition or multiple conceptions of spirituality and its association with religions could pose problems for academic research, professional dialogue and translation of ideas into practices but offer potentials for celebrating inclusivity of various cultural and religious traditions and embracing richness and depth. This echoes what Best's (2000, p. 10) analysis of the spiritual being 'most resistant to operational definition' (Adams, Bull, and Maynes 2016, p. 762). My predecessor, the former Director of Centre for Religious and Spiritual Education at The Education University of Hong Kong [formerly known as The Hong Kong Institute of Education], Ping-ho Wong (2006) asserts that spiritual education in schools is associated with the cultivation of students' moral values and virtues. With an educational research training and different sociocultural background myself and with a view of keeping the *IJCS* with a strong spiritual and religious foci, I try to broaden the scope of the Journal with the inclusion of life and values education as well as religious, philosophical, psychological and sociocultural perspectives and traditions both from and across the East and West. Hence, I have increased and will consider expanding gradually the editorial board membership of *IJCS*.

In an increasingly challenging, complicated and changing world, the moral, citizenship, spiritual and socio-emotional development of children and youngsters has attracted unprecedented global attention not only because it affects the well-being of individuals (Miller 2015, pp. 3–4) as future citizens and exerts a profound impact on an individual's whole-person development and late adulthood but it also has a significant influence on societal (re-)construction and nation-building. I personally have experienced deep feelings and reflections over the future of Hong Kong life, religious and values education and our children during the past few months in the Hong Kong Special Administrative Region of the People's Republic of China where there were social incidents and also affected by the recent outbreak of the novel coronavirus or COVID-19.

Paradoxically, while there are mounting challenges of children's well-being and mental health in many economically developed countries with an individualistic and materialistic culture, the spiritual dimension of childhood has not been given adequate attention in schools and universities where performance management and accountability prevail and educators and administrators are overloaded with tasks resulting probably in less personal touch and caring relationships with students (Adams 2017a, p. 1; Hyde, Watson, and Yust 2016).

Findings reveal that religious practices and habits could bring about better well-being and health for adolescents (Harvard Chan school of public health 2018, September 13). While spirituality and religions are to some extent associated and interrelated, the universal innate potentials of every individual with various background for spiritual development and transcendence experiences can be nurtured towards 'spiritual multi-lingualism' and harnessed both within and beyond the framework and practices of institutional religions (Miller 2015, pp. 191–193 & pp. 201–202; Collaborative for Spirituality in Education, u.d.).

Schools and schooling are probably one of the key platforms or processes through which young children encounter and engender spiritual and moral development. From the educational perspective, school education has a pivotal role to play in cultivating and facilitating young people to search and quest for the meaning of life as well as their personal recognition and self-actualisation (adapted from Crawford and Rossiter 2006, pp. 14–15). A language of spirituality, according to Crawford and Rossiter (2006, p. 9), is broad and inclusive. It is not only embracing a religious contribution but also incorporating a 'spiritual dimension to living that covers values, commitments and aesthetic concerns'.

de Souza (2016b, p. 132) remarked that a child is a 'multi-dimensional being; an individual with a rational mind that thinks, an emotional mind that feels and a spiritual mind that intuits, imagines, wonders and creates' (de Souza 2016a, p. 123). In addition, developing the innate capabilities and empowering the potentials of children will not only bring a positive impact on the well-being of future communities but also enhance their 'own sense of self, place and wellbeing' (de Souza 2016b, p. 134).

In Australia, the National Catholic Education Commission (2018, pp. 16–17) suggested that the Religious Education curriculum could help learners reflect on important questions such as 'who I am' and 'how I am' and their relations with God, the world and others as well as 'contribute to the common good' and other dispositions. This partly resonates the relationality of spirituality which pertains to relationality with self, others, the environment and the transcendent (Robinson 2017, pp. 30–38). This also echoes what Sun (2009, pp. 3–4) in Taiwan raises 'rensheng sanwen' three fundamental questions about life as an individual or human being pertaining to the reason we shall life, the meaning of live and the way we could live out (personal communication, May 2020).

From the perspective of educators promoting life education, we could perhaps provide responses on and take actions for stimulating and guiding children and learners: 1. to think about the questions about life, such as 'where am I coming from and going to?'; 2. to explore the meaning of their life; 3. to become a person with desirable qualities and competencies (e.g., to cultivate morality and virtues, to enhance spiritual and whole-person development, and to achieve unity of knowledge and action).

The connection with the environment may encompass elements of education for sustainability or sustainable education in the twenty-first century (de Souza 2016b; Lee and Efird 2014). All these multifaceted aspects or dimensions of life, spiritual and values education highlight that spirituality entails personal but not totally private experiences; it interacts relationally with and embeds an awareness of responsibility to self, others, the world and our nature (adapted from Cole 2011, p. 6).

There is thus a pressing need for the advocacy of promoting spirituality for young children and youngsters in different levels of education. However, the emphasis of spirituality, moral and values education may differ in different societies and contexts. Life education (Lau 2014; Lee and Kennedy 2019; Wong, Lee, Zhu, Ou et al. 2016) and moral and spirituality education are highlighted in schools, especially in the Greater China region. In Taiwan, there seems to be an emphasis on religious and spiritual practices related to ultimate concerns (Lau 2014, p. 174). There is also an advocacy of life and death education where students engage in experiential learning through field trips to hospices, interviews with relatives, observation of the life cycles of plants and animals in parks and zoos as well as small-group discussions with classmates (Lor 2018). In China, where religions are still under state control and partly because of the influence of Socialist and Maoist ideologies and now under the leadership of President Jinping Xi, there is no discernable religious aspect of spirituality in the curriculum (Lau 2014, p. 174). Instead, there is an emphasis on harmony, 'shengcun' (safety) and other core socialist values, some of which are based on Chinese traditional values under the influence of Confucianism (Gow 2017). Taking curriculum of 'sanshengjiaoyu' (Life, Live and Living Curriculum) as one of the examples or variants of life education in Mainland China, 'shengming' (life) education refers mainly to understanding the processes of life and death and respect of life (Lau 2014, p. 173). There could be ample opportunities for scholarly and professional exchanges between life education and religious education as there are a lot of remarkable programmes and research on children's perceptions of living and dying, especially based on Christian religious education in the West (Champagne 2008). In Japan where bullying is a serious problem, there has been an attention on teaching school children the importance of 'Inochi' (life) as 'education of the mind', and in the elementary school curriculum, there is moral education such as perceptions of 'preciousness of life' and 'importance of living things', while religious education is relatively less explicitly touched upon (Nakayama 2019, pp. 5/12 & 6/12).

In some cases, schools are considered as units of change, and taking the Collaborative for Spirituality in Education (u.d.) as an example, it is proposed that a spiritually supportive school would entail the following characteristics: respect and love; moral development; purpose and meaning; wonder; self-care and inner life; caring relationships; democracy and social justice; compassion and service; joy/ whole being; and connection to nature. Teachers are also key agents and role models for life and spiritual education. A research on teachers in elementary schools in 12 countries showed that a majority of respondents (around 76%) perceived spirituality as a way for children to develop their relationships and that the remainder (around 24%) regarded children's spirituality as an opportunity for transcendence and mysticism. As far as the opinions on values of education and spirituality are concerned, the results seemed to show a diversity ranging from the connections between various spirituality values through conformity of spiritual principles and values education (about 50%) to close association between spirituality and moral education (about 22%) and spirituality as universal core concept (about 27%). The findings also showed that teachers' views of spirituality for children's values education might hinge on their own spiritual experiences (Pandya 2017, pp. 36–37, p. 39). Spiritual development in education is easier to be said than done. There have been suggestions on helping children develop an open mind, explore their own way of seeing without social and mental conditioning and encourage personal awareness (Duff 2003, pp. 235–236; Hay and Nye 1998, pp. 155, 163–168).

Such school development including teacher and student development possibly not only calls for spiritual leadership (Tsui et al. 2019) but also necessitates teachers' continuous professional development in life and spiritual education, their sustained reflection on spiritual practices, valuing spiritual diversity and respect for human rights, other voices and perspectives as well as deep understanding of themselves and their students (Cole 2011, p. 10 & p. 13; Watson 2017, pp. 11–12). To conclude, it is desirable that three-pronged interactive and interdisciplinary approaches may be adopted for enhancing the spirituality area of children. The first approach is to study about children's spirituality through interdisciplinary research and development. The second approach is to work and learn with/from our children with innate capacities and unique qualities. The third approach is to contribute our research and development endeavours and experiences to the betterment and spiritual development of our children as whole persons. As editorial team colleagues, contributors and readers of *IJCS*, you are cordially invited and most welcome to continuously engage in academic and professional dialogues in the fields of spirituality, life, values and spiritual education about, with/from and for our whole children.

Note

1. W-t, Chan. (1963). Translation of Mengzi 4A:12, *A Source Book in Chinese Philosophy*. Princeton: Princeton University Press, p.74.

Acknowledgements

This article reflects the author's personal views only and does not necessarily represent the views of the UNESCO and The Education University of Hong Kong and does not commit the respective organisations.

Disclosure statement

No potential conflict of interest was reported by the author.

References

Adams, K. 2017a. "Towards an Interdisciplinary Approach to Understanding the Nurturing of Spirituality and the Whole Child." *International Journal of Children's Spirituality* 22 (1): 1–3. doi:10.1080/1364436X.2017.1279726.

Adams, K., R. Bull, and M.-L. Maynes. 2016. "Early Childhood Spirituality in Education: Towards an Understanding of the Distinctive Features of Young Children's Spirituality." *European Early Childhood Education Research Journal* 24 (5): 760–774. doi:10.1080/1350293X.2014.996425.

Best, R., Ed. 2000. *Education for Spiritual, Moral, Social and Cultural Development*. London: Continuum.

Champagne, E. 2008. "Living and Dying: A Window on (Christian) Children's Spirituality." *International Journal of Children's Spirituality* 13 (3): 253–263. doi:10.1080/13644360802236490.

Cole, S. 2011. "Situating Children in the Discourse of Spirituality." *Spirituality, Education & Society: An Integrated Approach*. edited by N. N. Wane, E. L. Manyimo, and E. J. Ritskes, 1–14. The Netherlands: Sense Publishers. https://www.springer.com/gp/book/9789460916038

Crawford, M., and G. Rossiter. 2006. *Reasons for Living: Education and Young People's Search for Meaning, Identity and Spirituality – A Handbook*. Camberwell, Victoria, Australia: ACER Press. https://search.informit.com.au/browsePublication;isbn=9780864316134;res=IELHSS

de Souza, M. 2016a. *Spirituality in Education in a Global, Pluralised World*. New York: Routledge. https://www.taylorfrancis.com/books/9781315752761

de Souza, M. 2016b. "The Spiritual Dimension of Education in Addressing Issues of Identity and Belonging." *Discourse and Communication for Sustainable Education* 7 (1): 125–138. doi:10.1515/dcse-2016-0009.

Department for Education, Employment and Workplace Relations (DEEWR). 2009. *Belonging, Being and Becoming: The Early Years Learning Framework for Australia*. Canberra: Commonwealth of Australia. https://www.acecqa.gov.au/sites/default/files/2018-02/belonging_being_and_becoming_the_early_years_learning_framework_for_australia.pdf

Duff, L. 2003. "Spiritual Development and Education: A Contemplative View." *International Journal of Children's Spirituality* 8 (3): 227–237. doi:10.1080/13644360032000146502.

Eaude, T. 2019. "The Role of Culture and Traditions in How Young Children's Identities are Constructed." *International Journal of Children S Spirituality* 24 (1): 1–15. doi:10.1080/1364436X.2019.1619534.

Giesenberg, A. 2007. "The Phenomenon of Preschool Children's Spirituality." PhD unpublished dissertation, Queensland University of Technology, Australia.

Gow, M. 2017. "The Core Socialist Values of the Chinese Dream: Towards a Chinese Integral State." *Critical Asian Studies* 49 (1): 92–116. doi:10.1080/14672715.2016.1263803.

Harvard, T. H., Chan School of Public Health. 2018, September 13. "News: Religious Upbringing Linked to Better Health and Well-being during Early Adulthood". Accessed 28 September 2019 https://www.hsph.harvard.edu/news/press-releases/religious-upbringing-adult-health/

Hay, D., and R. Nye. 1998. *The Spirit of the Child*. London: Harper Collins.

Hyde, B., J. Watson, and K. M. Yust. 2016. "'Brexit Spirituality' – The Complex (and Not so Complex) Withdrawal of Spirituality from the Curriculum." *International Journal of Children's Spirituality* 21: 3–4. doi:10.1080/1364436X.2016.1232517.

Lau, N. S. E. 2014. "Life Education in Contemporary Chinese Societies." In *Global Perspectives on Spirituality and Education*, edited by J. Watson, M. de Souza, and A. Trousdale, 166–180. New York: Routledge.

Lee, J. C. K., and K. J. Kennedy, Eds. 2019. *The Routledge Series on Life and Values Education*. U. K.: Routledge. https://www.routledge.com/Routledge-Series-on-Life-and-Values-Education /book-series/RSLVE

Lee, J. C. K., and R. Efird, Eds. 2014. *Schooling for Development across the Pacific*. The Netherlands: Springer.

Lor, J. 2018. *Death Education Is Life Education*. Institute of Policy Studies (IPS) Commons. Accessed 16 October 2019. https://www.ipscommons.sg/death-education-is-life-education/

Love, P. G. 2001. "Spirituality and Student Development: Theoretical Connections." *New Directions for Student Services* 95 (Autumn (Fall)): 7–16. https://onlinelibrary.wiley.com/doi/pdf/10.1002/ss.18

Miller, L. 2015. *The Spiritual Child: The New Science on Parenting for Health and Lifelong Thriving*. U.S.: St. Martin's Press.

Myers, K. B. 1997. *Young Children and Spirituality*. New York: Routledge.

Nakayama, O. 2019. "New Spirituality in Japan and Its Place in the Teaching of Moral Education." *Religions* 10: 278. doi:10.3390/rel10040278.

National Catholic Education Commission. 2018. *Framing Paper: Religious Education in Australian Catholic Schools*. Sydney, Australia: NCEC. https://www.ncec.catholic.edu.au/images/NCEC_Framing_Paper_Religious_Education.pdf

Pandya, S. P. 2017. "Spirituality and Values Education in Elementary School: Understanding Views of Teachers." *Children & Schools* 39 (1): 33–41. doi:10.1093/cs/cdw042.

Chan, W-t. (1963). Translation of Mengzi 4A:12, A Source Book in Chinese Philosophy. Princeton: Princeton University Press, p.74.

Robinson, C. 2017. "Educators' Practices for Promoting the Spiritual Development of Children Aged 3 to 4 Years, in the Context of Catholic Childcare Centres in Western Australia." Unpublished Doctor of Philosophy (College of Education)thesis. University of Notre Dame Australia. https://researchonline.nd.edu.au/theses/159

Rossiter, G. 2011. "Reorienting the Religion Curriculum in Catholic Schools to Address the Needs of Contemporary Youth Spirituality." *International Studies in Catholic Education* 3 (1): 57–72. doi:10.1080/19422539.2011.540140.

Selvam, S. 2013. "Towards Religious-spirituality: A Multi-dimensional Matrix of Religion and Spirituality." *Journal of the Study of Religions and Ideologies* 12 (36): 129–152.

Sun, H.-C. 2009. "Challenges and Visions – Life Education in Taiwan." *Curriculum and Instruction Quarterly [Taiwan Shengming Jiaoyu De Tiaozhan Yu Yuanjing. Kecheng Yu Jiaoxue Jikan]* 12 (3): 1–26.

Tisdell, E. 2003. "Breaking the Silence: Defining Spirituality and Culture Identity in Transformative Adult Higher Education." *Journal of Transformative Education* 1 (4): 368–392. doi:10.1177/1541344603257678.

Tsui, K. T., J. C. K. Lee, Z. Zhang, and P. H. Wong. 2019. "The Relationship between Teachers' Perceived Spiritual Leadership and Organizational Commitment: A Multi-level Analysis in the Hong Kong Context." *Asian Journal of Social Sciences & Humanities (AJSSH), Japan* 8 (3): 55–72. http://www.ajssh.leena-luna.co.jp/AJSSHPDFs/Vol.8(3)/AJSSH2019(8.3-06).pdf

Van der Zee, T., and K. Tirri. 2009. "Research on Religious and Spiritual Education: Guest Editorial." *Journal of Empirical Theology* 22 (1): 1–6. doi:10.1163/157092509X437189.

Watson, J. 2017. "Every Child Still Matters: Interdisciplinary Approaches to the Spirituality of the Child." *International Journal of Children's Spirituality* 22 (1): 4–13. doi:10.1080/1364436X.2016.1234434.

Wills, R., A. Gellel, and K.-M. Yust. 2018a. "Evolving Editorial Roles: Introducing the New Team." *International Journal of Children's Spirituality* 23 (1): 1–2. doi:10.1080/1364436X.2018.1441641.

Wong, P. H. 2006. "A Conceptual Investigation into the Possibility of Spiritual Education." *International Journal of Children's Spirituality* 11 (1)): 73–85. doi:10.1080/13644360500503407.

Wong, Lee, Zhu, Ou et al.,, et al. Eds. 2016. *Life Education: Its Intellectual, Emotional, Volitional and Practical Dimensions*. New Taipei City, Taiwan: Yang-Chih Book Co., [in Chinese].

Introduction (2 of 2)— Children's spirituality, life and religious education: socio-cultural and religious traditions and perspectives

John Chi-Kin Lee

An individual's spiritual development, as proposed by some scholars (adapted from Benson 2006, 489; Roehlkepartain 2014, 10) and from a socio-ecological perspective (King and Boyatzis 2004, 2015), is influenced by and interacts with culture (including language, norms, customs, etc.) and social contexts such as family, school, religious communities, peers, media and so on as well as shaped by significant life experiences over time, and creating and inheriting narratives, myths and interpretative frameworks about what is good and important, ideal life and person and the reality, all of which echo and address an individual's meaning and purpose of life, moral duty and personal motivation to realise one's life values and make contribution to the family, society, nation and the world. Within this framework, there are a range of sociological constructs that could assist us to make sense of changes in spirituality. These constructs include those related to religion and change (e.g., secularisation, world views, religiosity), pertaining to social change (e.g., individualism, pluralism, cultural postmodernity, relativism, intercultural communication), associated with institutional change (e.g., de-institutionalisation), related to social psychological constructs (e.g., identity, meaning and purpose, wellbeing, character and virtues) (Rossiter 2010, 132–134). In addition, there are a spectrum and a variety of models of spiritual development ranging from traditional models that include indigenous models, Western models and Eastern religious models to integrative-philosophical models and psychological models entailing psychology of religion, transpersonal psychology and neurobiological models (Friedman et al. 2012, 210–217). Apart from the well-established Western religious models and research-based Western, psychological models of spirituality, there could be insights drawn from the indigenous models and Eastern religious models. In a review of instruments on indigenous spirituality and resilience in the context of Indigenous/First Nations communities in North America, the components of enculturation maintaining bicultural characteristics and cultural spiritual orientation were identified. This review suggested that Aboriginal spirituality could serve as a resource for life education and for transcendence (Fleming and Ledogar 2008). In addition, a recent document in Canada recommended the development of Indigenous-specific early childhood education training programme taking into account Indigenous worldviews and indigenous languages (Halseth and Greenwood 2019, 53; Inuit Tapiriit Kanatami, 2014). There are also discussions on shamanism as one of the examples of indigenous models of spiritual development which is conducive to spiritual healing and therapy (Eliade and Diószegi 2017; Friedman et al. 2012, 210–211; Vadala 2019).

Different major religious traditions have diverse views and enriched wisdom on children and adolescent's spirituality. The Hindu tradition considers the One Supreme Being takes the forms of children as gods and goddesses underpinned by the concept of latent spirituality of children and the Guru is expected to be the teacher who guides children to develop their spirituality (Agarwal, 2006, 19, 24; Yust et al. 2006, 15). The Muslim understanding of children and adolescent's spirituality, as shown in the Qur'an and Islamic teachings related to Prophet Muhammad, children are seen as 'gifts from Allah' and children are expected to join in adults' Muslim spiritual practices and learn about the concepts of mercy, love, respect and trust (Yildirim 2006, 69–70, 78–79; Yust et al. 2006, 17).

Religious education and its impact on children and adolescent's spirituality and life values development travel across geographical boundaries. Taking Catholic education as an example, while it has originated in the West and influence worldwide, the transcendental nature of Catholic education in Taiwan was reflected in the establishment of Religious Counselling and Life Education office for spirituality education and the implementation of 'Holistic Education' where morality and personality were emphasised in the pedagogical approach (Lin 2013; Lin and Leung 2018, 157). Such ideas and practices of life education in Catholic schools were later spread to some other Taiwan schools becoming part of the school curriculum (Yage 2012; Lee 2020). Another example is the comparison of Christian and Buddhist preschools in Japan where it depicts the influences of different religious traditions on preschool education. It is interesting to note that Christian preschools tended to encourage children's exploration and creativity while Buddhist preschools highlighted the importance of cultivation of children's virtues, cognitive stimulation and physical development (Holloway 1999). Children' different religious experiences and religious influences on kindergarten are also discerned in two kindergartens, one Catholic and one Islamic, in the same district of Vienna, Austria. These different cases pinpointed the need to examine whether every child has the right of equal opportunities to develop his/her spirituality and whether quality and safe spaces could be provided to children (Stockinger 2019, 309, 313–315; Nye 2017, 8).

Understanding children's spirituality needs to understand and assess what and how children create meaning, construct their identities (Eaude 2019) and perceive spirituality. Adams (2019) studied the divine dream of more than 500 United Kingdom children aged 9–12 from Muslim, and Christian secular backgrounds. It was noticeable that children's dream imagery reflected religious beliefs being aligned with the child's respective cultural background: Muslim children's dreams with mosques only while church only appeared in Christian or secular children's dreams. Hyde (2008) study in Australia, however, demonstrated that there could be either intersection or hybridisation of different the secular and/or religious traditions and 'spiritual-but-not-religious' (e.g., mindfulness, 'new age' and the idea of 'mind, body, spirit') (Adams 2019, 36). From a research perspective, it is cautionary to note that it may be desirable to dig deep into not only children's own spiritual images, meaning and content of theologies but also how children create such children's theologies as phenomena both individually and collectively (adapted from Csinos 2018, 53).

There have been international studies revealing the positive association between adolescent religiosity and their psychosocial functioning (Stolz et al. 2013). While we note children's spirituality is to some extent linked with their religious affiliation and experiences, religious education might also have encountered changes in contemporary societies. Rossiter (2010) highlighted that Catholic schools in Australia tended to undergo changes towards more 'secular, eclectic and individualistic' trends. On the other hand, parents as one of a significant others and parental religiousness may have some influence on child's spiritual development and adjustment such as social competence and school performance. Bornstein et al. (2017, 1–2, 10) study revealed that with a few exceptions, parental religiousness might have positive or negative associations dependent on the association with parental efficacy (positive) or parental control (negative) with child adjustment across nine sites in different countries. In addition, parental religiousness and parental efficacy tended to be more significant for Italian and Catholics groups (p.12). Another study found that there were different types of religious parenting under the Finnish context of Orthodox Christian tradition as a minority depending on whether parents were insecure, moderate or passionate who might exert some impact in religious upbringings of their children (Metso 2018, 20)

From a religious learning and psychological perspective, there has been an interest to explore whether a child could cognitively develop spirituality from a very young age. Fowler (1981) proposed a faith development theory and suggested when a child matures, he/she could have better ability in spiritual awareness and engagement. Along a similar line of thinking, Hart (2003) considered that while a child could have access to spirituality throughout his/her development, spirituality is relatively at the higher level of development, implying some potential limitations for young child's development (Moore et al. 2016, 2/11). On the other hand, Boyatzis (2012) argued that children are 'spiritual beings first' (153). King and Boyatzis (2004), King and Boyatzis (2015) further proposed from a socio-ecological perspective that children are capable of having awareness and understanding of their relationship with a divine entity at a very early age and before exposing to 'religious socialisation' (Boyatzis 2012, 153). Another line of thinking and discourses is whether interreligious learning is relevant, desirable and feasible in Catholic Religious Education for very young children. It has been asserted that for some scholars, for example, Dillen (2015, 156 & 162) in the Flemish context, children like adults are capable and competent to 'have a vision on faith and life' and interreligious learning allows children to engage in religious communication under the context of a 'dialogue [Catholic] school'.

In measuring children's spirituality, a measure was developed in Canada with three factors: Comfort; Omnipresence; and Duality (Moore et al. 2016, 6–7/11). The factor of Comfort refers to God as an important origin of support and comfort. The factor of Omnipresence is related to God as 'an omnipresent being and creator of the world' (Moore et al. 2016). The factor of Duality entails the notion of having a spirit or a soul apart from the body. These findings revealed that children might have the ability and potential of understanding the preliminary idea of transcendence and distinguishing between human and divine signs (7–8/11). From a spiritual or life education perspective, children could be encouraged or facilitated in activities that are conducive to spiritual engagement. There are other measures and studies of children's spirituality such as Expressions of Spirituality Inventory–Revised based on the transpersonal perspective (Mendez and MacDonald 2017) as well as the longitudinal study of middle-school Israeli adolescents which revealed that spirituality being an autonomous factor was stable over time and was conducive to higher subjective well-being and prosociality (Kor et al. 2019, 1). Nonetheless, it is mindful that not every aspect of spirituality such as the joy and wonder of art and nature could be easily measured (Lunn 2018, 38; Hay and Nye 2006). Evidence of empowering children's spiritual voices based on freedom and autonomy as well as creating relational and other spaces (Adams 2019, 40–41; Nye 2017, 8) are valuable for life, religious and spirituality education which may not be compatible with the demands of external accountability based on numbers and quantifiable improvements instead of individual's experiences and stories.

Apart from measurement and assessment of spirituality, there are different educational and curriculum approaches that could possibly nurture children's spirituality. However, there have been variations and tensions of religious and values education in different societies and contexts. In the United States, there have been advocacy of caring ethics and exploration of existential issues in the classroom (Noddings 1992, 2008), the launch of the Bible Literacy Project (http://www.bibleliteracy.org/; Ryan 2019) as well as discussions of multiculturalism (Banks and McGee Banks 2007) and critiques on misrepresentation of Muslims and Islam in social studies textbooks (Jackson 2010, 2011; Rosenblith 2017, 8–9/18). Eaude (2006, 22) remarked that children could be nurtured to 'search, question and reflect' through spiritual development (Lunn 2018, 32) and he further (Eaude 2019, 6) suggested that apprenticeship and holistic approaches might be conducive to children's spirituality. Teachers were encouraged to engage students in challenging or questioning messages from the macro-culture which might emphasise individualism and consumerism as well as their own cultural traditions while being respectful, appreciative of and sensitive to the latter.

An education programme (adapted from Egan (2001, 6–7)) based on Plato's belief and a philosophical approach could encourage children to challenge and question their beliefs about the world and their own spiritual experiences, appreciate other people's human experiences and the linkage between the past and present and introduce to them various scholarly virtues such as precision and caution and self-sacrifice for the good of others. Other approaches encompass the use of stories, learning of indigenous beliefs, contact and connection with nature and others as well as engagement of children in the discussion of the nature of existence (Vialle, Walton, and Woodcock 2008, 149–150). Spirituality, to some extent, has connections with holistic art education which touches upon the promotion 'of spirituality and life, for awareness, awakening, and enlightenment' (Liu 2012, 65, 2013, 64) as well as cultivation of spiritual intelligence based on the concepts such as mindfulness and concentration, empathy and sympathy and play (Liu 2013, 62–63). For music, it has also links with spirituality in music therapy (Tsiris 2018). In any case, we could not simply assume that children accept good values set uncritically and passively and that teachers as reflective practitioners are encouraged to adopt balancing and respectful acts towards different socio-cultural and religious traditions (Carroll 2009, 126; Eaude 2006, 20, 76).

Based on the above limited snapshots, it seems that under a changing and dynamic world, we need to conduct more systematic, representative and longitudinal studies (Roehlkepartain 2014, 17) as well as three types of foundational, applied and contextualised research on spirituality (Ubani and Murtonen 2018, 103–104) using diverse methodologies to inform and unpack the essential factors and elements affecting children's spirituality. While we note there could be socio-cultural contexts and religious variations that could impact children's and individual spirituality, searching for commonalities and not be overridden by the stereotypes or schisms such as West-East dichotomy, cultures of individualism and collectivism and self and other is important (Vialle, Walton, and Woodcock 2008, 143). The findings from these studies could inspire the academia and professional fields and provide profound implications for life, spiritual, values and religious education at the levels of schools, communities and for national policies and global agenda for enhancing children's spirituality.

Acknowledgments

This article reflects the author's personal views only and does not necessarily represent the views of the UNESCO and the Education University of Hong Kong and does not commit the respective organisations.

Disclosure statement

No potential conflict of interest was reported by the author.

References

Adams, K. 2019. "Navigating the Spaces of Children's Spiritual Experiences: Influences of Tradition(s), Multidisciplinarity and Perceptions." *International Journal of Children's Spirituality* 24 (1): 29–43. doi:10.1080/1364436X.2019.1619531.

Agarwal, V. 2006. "Awakening Latent Spirituality: Nurturing Children in the Hindu Tradition." In *Nurturing Child and Adolescent Spirituality: Perspectives from the World's Religious Traditions*, edited by K. M. Yust, A. N. Johnson, S. E. Sasso, and E. C. Roehlkepartain, 19–32. Oxford, UK: Rowman & Littlefield Publishers.

Banks, J. A., and C. A. McGee Banks. 2007. *Multicultural Education: Issues and Perspectives*. 4th ed. Hoboken, NJ: Wiley.

Benson, P. L. 2006. "The Science of Child and Adolescent Spiritual Development: Definitional, Theoretical, and Field-building Challenges." In *The Handbook of Spiritual Development in Childhood and Adolescence*, edited by E. C. Roehlkepartain, P. E. King, L. Wagener, and P. L. Benson, 484–497. Thousand Oaks, CA: Sage.

Bornstein, M. H., D. L. Putnick, J. E. Lansford, S. M. Al-Hassan, D. Bacchini, A. S. Bombi, L. Chang, et al. 2017. "'Mixed Blessings': Parental Religiousness, Parenting, and Child Adjustment in Global Perspective." *The Journal of Child Psychology and Psychiatry* 58 (8): 880–892. doi:10.1111/jcpp.12705.

Boyatzis, C. 2012. "Spiritual Development during Childhood and Adolescence." In *The Oxford Handbook of Psychology and Spirituality*, edited by L. Miller, 151–164. New York: Oxford University Press.

Carroll, M. 2009. "Book Review: Children's Spiritual, Moral, Social and Cultural Development: Primary and Early Years." *Journal of Moral Education* 38 (1): 125–128. doi:10.1080/03057240802636934.

Csinos, D. M. 2018. "From the Ground Up: Cultural Considerations in Research into Children's Spirituality and Theology." *International Journal of Children's Spirituality* 23 (1): 53–66. doi:10.1080/1364436X.2017.1394271.

Dillen, A. 2015. "Aren't They Too Young? The Challenge of Hermeneutical and Interreligious Learning in Catholic Religious Education: A Flemish Perspective." In *Global Perspectives on Catholic Religious Education in Schools*, edited by Michael T. Buchanan, and Adrian-Mario Gellel, 155–165. Singapore: Springer.

Eaude, T. 2006. *Children's Spiritual, Moral, Social and Cultural Development: Primary and Early Years*. Exeter, UK: Learning Matters.

Eaude, T. 2019. "The Role of Culture and Traditions in How Young Children's Identities are Constructed." *International Journal of Children's Spirituality* 24 (1): 5–19. doi:10.1080/1364436X.2019.1619534.

Egan, K. 2001. "Spirituality, Education and the Moral Life." The American Educational Research Association conference, Seattle, WA, April 10. Accessed 21 October 2019. https://www.sfu.ca/~egan/AERA-Spirituality.html

Eliade, M., and V. Diószegi. 2017. "Shamanism." In Encyclopedia Britannica. Accessed 22 October 2019. https://www.britannica.com/topic/shamanism

Fleming, J., and R. J. Ledogar. 2008. "Resilience and Indigenous Spirituality: A Literature Review." *Pimatisiwin* 6 (2): 47–64.

Fowler, J. 1981. *Stages of Faith: The Psychology of Human Development and the Quest for Meaning*. San Francisco, CA: Harper & Row.

Friedman, H., S. Krippner, L. Riebel, and C. Johnson. 2012. "Models of Spiritual Development." In *The Oxford Handbook of Psychology and Spirituality*, edited by L. Miller, 207–220. New York: Oxford University Press.

Halseth, R., and M. Greenwood. 2019. *Indigenous Early Childhood Development in Canada: Current State of Knowledge and Future Directions*. Prince George, BC: National Collaborating Centre for Aboriginal Health. https://www.nccah-ccnsa.ca/docs/health/RPT-ECD-PHAC-Greenwood-Halseth-EN.pdf

Hart, T. 2003. *The Secret Spiritual World of Children*. Novato, CA: New World Library.

Hay, D., and R. Nye. 2006. *The Spirit of the Child*. rev ed. London, UK: Harper Collins.

Holloway, S. D. 1999. "The Role of Religious Beliefs in Early Childhood Education: Christian and Buddhist Preschools in Japan." *Early Childhood Research & Practice* 1 (2). http://ecrp.uiuc.edu/v1n2/holloway.html

Hyde, B. 2008. *Children and Spirituality: Searching for Meaning and Connectedness*. London, UK: Jessica Kingsley.

Inuit Tapiriit Kanatami [ITK]. 2014. "Assessing the Impact of the First Nations and Inuit Child Care Initiative (FNICCI) across Inuit Nunangat." https://www.itk.ca/wp-content/uploads/2016/07/2014_Report_FNICCI_Impacts_Inuit_Nunangat.pdf

Jackson, L. 2010. "Images of Islam in US Media and Their Educational Implications." *Educational Studies* 46 (1): 17. doi:10.1080/00131940903480217.

Jackson, L. 2011. "Islam and Muslims in U.S. Public Schools since September 11, 2001." *Religious Education* 196 (2): 173.

King, P. E., and C. J. Boyatzis. 2004. "Exploring Adolescent Spiritual and Religious Development: Current and Future Theoretical and Empirical Perspectives." *Applied Developmental Science* 8 (1): 2–6. doi:10.1207/S1532480XADS0801_1.

King, P. E., and C. J. Boyatzis. 2015. "Religious and Spiritual Development in Childhood and Adolescence." In *The Handbook of Child Psychology and Developmental Science (7th Ed.)*, edited by M. Lamb, C. Coll, and R. Lerner, 975–1021. Hoboken, NJ: Wiley.

Kor, A., S. Pirutinsky, M. Mikulincer, A. Shoshani, and L. Miller. 2019. "A Longitudinal Study of Spirituality, Character Strengths, Subjective Well-being, and Prosociality in Middle School Adolescents." *Frontiers in Psychology* 10 (Article): 377. doi:10.3389/fpsyg.2019.00377.

Lee, J. C. K. 2020. "Editorial: Children's Spirituality, Life and Values Education: Cultural, Spiritual and Educational Perspectives." *International Journal of Children's Spirituality* 25 (1): 1–8. doi:10.1080/1364436X.2020.1790774.

Lin, P. Y. T., and B. K. F. Leung. 2018. "Taiwan Catholic Higher Education: Is Contribution to the Greater China Region." In *The Catholic Church in Taiwan: Birth, Growth and Development*, edited by F. K. H. So, B. K. F. Leung, and E. M. Mylod, 153–177. Singapore: Palgrave Macmillan.

Lin, Y. T. 2013. *The Open Thinking in Catholic Higher Education*. Taiwan: Window Press. [in Chinese].

Liu, F. J. 2012. "Spirituality in Art and the Values of Spirituality Oriented Holistic Art Education." In *Proceedings of Conference of New Spirituality in Post-modern Art*, 1st ed., 52–63. Chiayi, Taiwan: National Chiayi University. (in Chinese).

Liu, F. J. 2013. "Theoretical Foundations for Spirituality-oriented Holistic Art Education: Integration of Eastern and Western Aesthetics." In *Creative Arts in Education and Culture: Perspectives from Greater China*, edited by S. Leong and B. W. Leung, 55–67. The Netherlands: Springer.

Lunn, A. 2018. "A Critical Analysis of the Role of Spirituality within the Early Years Curriculum." *Transformation* 1: 27–41.

Mendez, D. M., and D. A. MacDonald. 2017. "The Measurement of Spirituality in Children: An Evaluation of the Expressions of Spirituality Inventory–Revised (ESI–R) with a Sample of Peruvian School Children." *International Journal of Transpersonal Studies* 36 (1). doi:10.24972/ijts.2017.36.1.122.

Metso, P. 2018. "Raising a Christian or an Orthodox Christian: Parents' Experience of Their Ecumenical Reality and Minority Status in the Religious Upbringing of Finnish Orthodox Children and Youth." In *New International Studies on Religions and Dialogue in Education*, edited by M. Urbani, 13–30. Germany and New York: Waxmann Verlag.

Moore, K., C. Gomez-Garibello, S. Bosacki, and V. Talwar. 2016. "Children's Spiritual Lives: The Development of a Children's Spirituality Measure." *Religions* 7 (8): 95. doi:10.3390/rel7080095.

Noddings, N. 1992. *The Challenge to Care in Schools: An Alternative Approach to Education*. New York: Teachers College Press.

Noddings, N. 2008. "Chapter 13: Spirituality and Religion in Public Schooling." *Yearbook of the National Society for the Study of Education* 107 (1): 185–195. doi:10.1111/j.1744-7984.2008.00141.x.

Nye, R. 2017. "Spirituality as a Natural Part of Childhood." *Transmission, Spring*, 5–8. https://www.biblesociety.org.uk/content/explore_the_bible/bible_in_transmission/files/2017_spring_v2/transmission_spring_2017_nye.pdf

Roehlkepartain, E. C. 2014. "Children, Religion, and Spiritual Development: Reframing a Research Agenda." In *The SAGE Handbook of Child Research*, edited by G. B. Melton, A. Ben-Arieh, J. Cashmore, G. S. Goodman, and N. K. Worley, 81–99. London: SAGE Publications.

Rosenblith, S. 2017. "Religion in Schools in the United States." *Oxford Research Encyclopedia*. Subject: Education and Society. U.S.A.: Oxford University Press.

Rossiter, G. 2010. "Perspective on Contemporary Spirituality: Implications for Religious Education in Catholic Schools." *International Studies in Catholic Education* 2 (2): 129–147. doi:10.1080/19422539.2010.504019.

Ryan, E. 2019. "There's a Push for Classes on the Bible in Public Schools. And There's Also a Pushback." CNN, May 7. https://edition.cnn.com/2019/05/06/politics/bible-literacy-classes-legislation/index.html

Stockinger, H. 2019. "Developing Spirituality – An Equal Right of Every Child?" *International Journal of Children's Spirituality* 24 (3): 307–319. doi:10.1080/1364436X.2019.1646218.

Stolz, H. E., J. A. Olsen, T. M. Henke, and B. K. Barber. 2013. "Adolescent Religiosity and Psychosocial Functioning: Investigating the Roles of Religious Tradition, National-ethnic Group, and Gender." *Child Development Research* 13. Article ID 814059. doi: 10.1155/2013/814059.

Tsiris, G. 2018. "Performing Spirituality in Music Therapy: Towards Action, Context and the Everyday." Unpublished PhD thesis, Nordoff Robbins/ Goldsmiths,University of London United Kingdom. http://research.gold.ac.uk/23037/1/MUS_thesis_TsirisG_2018.pdf

Ubani, M., and S. Murtonen. 2018. "Editorial: Issues in Spiritual Formation in Early Lifespan Contexts." *International Journal of Children's Spirituality* 23 (2): 103–108. doi:10.1080/1364436X.2018.1452557.

Vadala, J. 2019. "Cross-culturally Exploring the Concept of Shamanism." Human Relations Area Files (HRAF), Yale University, Cultural information for education and research. Accessed 22 October 2019. https://hraf.yale.edu/cross-culturally-exploring-the-concept-of-shamanism/

Vialle, W., R. Walton, and S. Woodcock. 2008. "Children's Spirituality: An Essential Element in Thinking and Learning in New Times." In *Learning and the Learner: Exploring Learning for New Times*, edited by P. Kell, W. Vialle, D. Konza, and G. Vogl, 143–160. Wollongong, NSW: University of Wollongong Press.

Yage, X. 2012. "Taiwan, Catholic Schools Reference Points for Real 'Life Education'." AsiaNews, October 31. Accessed 23 October 2019. http://www.asianews.it/news-en/Taiwan,-Catholic-schools-reference-points-for-real-life-education-26234.html

Yildirim, Y. 2006. "Filling the Heart with the Love of God: Islamic Perspectives on Spirituality in Childhood and Adolescence." In *Nurturing Child and Adolescent Spirituality: Perspectives from the World's Religious Traditions*, edited by K. M. Yust, A. N. Johnson, S. E. Sasso, and E. C. Roehlkepartain, 69–80. Oxford, UK: Rowman & Littlefield Publishers.

Yust, K. M., A. N. Johnson, S. E. Sasso, and E. C. Roehlkepartain, Eds. 2006. *Nurturing Child and Adolescent Spirituality: Perspectives from the World's Religious Traditions*. Oxford, UK: Rowman & Littlefield Publishers.

Preparing spirituality for citizenship

Jacqueline Watson

ABSTRACT
Schools in England and Wales are responsible for the spiritual development of pupils and, since 2002, for the citizenship education of secondary school pupils. However, despite many government documents and much academic discussion, it is still not clear what spirituality means for schools and citizenship looks to be an equally problematic concept. This article sets out to do two things. First, it reports on a 'survey' of a bounded sample group of academic articles, namely those which have appeared in the International Journal of Children's Spirituality, for academics' understandings of the meaning of spirituality for schools. Second, the article attempts to demonstrate a shift in the academic understanding of spirituality which may have left spirituality better prepared to co-exist with the new citizenship education, but which may also make it too hot for citizenship to handle.

Introduction

Spirituality and Citizenship for Schools

The most recent National Curriculum Handbook for England says the school curriculum has two aims. The first is to enable pupils to learn and achieve. The second is 'to promote pupils' spiritual, moral, social and cultural development and prepare all pupils for the opportunities, responsibilities and experiences of life'

'[which includes, for instance, helping] them to be responsible and caring citizens capable of contributing to the development of a just society' (DfEE & QCA, 1999, p. 11). This article is concerned with the second curriculum aim and is about spirituality and citizenship for schools.

There is a lack of certainty about what the words 'spirituality' and 'citizenship' are intended to mean in schools. In the case of citizenship this is partly because Citizenship Education is new: it became a statutory requirement for the secondary school curriculum in September 2002. Spirituality, however, has been a statutory part of the curriculum since 1944 and, although Ofsted (Office for Standards in Education) has inspected spiritual development in schools since 1993, even they give mixed messages about its meaning (Watson, 2000). It is sometimes argued that spirituality resists definition because it is 'elusive'. This article describes an analysis of academic definitions of spirituality which set out to penetrate that elusiveness. In the process, the analysis discovered potential for a close relationship between spirituality and citizenship; but it also found potential for considerable friction.

A Methodology for 'Defining' Spirituality

> It is in the nature of spirituality to be elusive. Whilst some teachers want to be clearer on what it is in order to 'teach it better', others strongly resist giving it a definition at all, knowing the tyrannical, restrictive power of definitions (Taggart, 2001, p. 323).

I suspect most teachers interested in spirituality recognise the fact that you do not 'teach' spirituality, but teachers might nonetheless benefit from greater clarity about what it is. Can spirituality be defined? I doubt it, but not because it has an elusive, whimsical and playful nature. Following Wittgenstein's line of argument—that words derive meaning from their use—it should be possible, at least in principle, to derive the meaning of the word 'spirituality' from its use. 'Spirituality' appears elusive because it now encompasses so many uses; all the more reason for attempting greater clarity about the meaning we have given it for schools. William Kay has said, in the absence of a clear understanding, 'the meaning of "spirituality" in any given context will be dependent upon the philosophical and theological framework of the writer' (Kay, 1996, p. 18). Reading the academic literature on spiritual development has often left me with the impression this was precisely what was happening but I did not find this helpful. Terence Copley (2000) and Clive Erricker's (Erricker & Erricker, 2000) recent overviews of the main trends in thinking about spirituality for schools are extremely helpful, but reinforce the impression of multiple meanings. I felt it would be useful to carry out a 'survey' of the academic literature to try to find our whether this impression would be sustained on close examination. I had anticipated little agreement, but I found more than I had expected. The title of this article reflects the story I felt emerged from the analytical process.

My survey set out to make a detailed comparative study of academic articles to see whether there was any agreement on the meaning of spirituality for schools, and where any agreement lay. My intention was to make an empirical study rather than a philosophical one. I wanted a bounded set of data as a sample group of academic views. For the sample group, I turned to the *International Journal of Children's Spirituality* (IJCS). I went through all editions of the IJCS, from its inauguration to the time of writing, Volume 1(1) to Volume 7(1), and drew out those articles which give an account of spirituality. This amounted to a total of 44 articles (not all of which are referred to in this article). Each of these articles was read, but definitions or descriptions of spirituality were extracted and analysed closely and mapped for shared themes, ideas and concerns, as well as major differences. The map formed the basis for what follows here, a fleshing back out of those themes, ideas and concerns which thus appeared to me to encompass the academic view of spirituality for schools.

I have tried to avoid comment on authors' arguments and views and looked only at how they defined or described spirituality. A number of the IJCS authors have written extensively on the subject elsewhere but I have not included that work here.

The articles were complex and usually developed arguments that went far beyond the immediate concerns of this article but I have not included those extended arguments either. I recognise this might amount to a reductive education approach. However, it was intended as a well-meaning attempt to seek clarification.

The article looks first at how spirituality was defined or described. It then looks at where it was located in the curriculum, which includes a discussion of affective and cognitive approaches to spiritual development in Religious Education. In moving beyond RE to the wider curriculum, the article explores the links with personal and moral development and finally with citizenship. I found spirituality had gone through something of a process of transformation over the years which might make it better prepared to take a seat under the new citizenship banner. However, I have concluded this may not be a comfortable arrangement: this depends on the way education for citizenship shapes up. Since Citizenship Education is a new phenomenon, it is as yet unclear exactly what form it will take (Watson, 2003) and there is an emerging debate about what form it *should* take (Jackson, 2003). In this article I have not felt able to attempt a detailed and explicit discussion of Citizenship Education. The article's main focus is spirituality. However, it is hoped the linkage with citizenship might prompt further debate.

One final note, on referencing: a large number of IJCS articles are used, and often used repeatedly. Therefore, for neatness in the text, I have used conventional referencing only where an IJCS author has more than one article in the journal, or to indicate page numbers for quotations.

Defining and Describing Spirituality

A Common Spirituality

Most IJCS authors shared the belief that spirituality is common to humanity and therefore to all children. It is inclusive. Sometimes this was assumed but often it was clearly stated, in particular by David Hay who has long argued spirituality is naturalistic and has evolved biologically because it is vital to human survival. Hay also points to 'a common concern for shared spiritual values' among religious believers and secularists as evidence for 'a common spirituality' (Hay, 1997, pp. 8–9).

Clive Erricker and Jerome Berryman share Hay's assumption of an innate childhood spirituality: for instance, Berryman says children 'cannot help but absorb the world about them naturally by contemplation' (p. 10). It is difficult to tell how far other authors would agree, but there is much agreement on the inclusivity of spirituality. This is sometimes implied through the humanness of authors' understanding of spirituality. For instance, Sandra Bosacki understands spirituality as inner meaning and emotion; Christopher Clouder links it with relationship; Geoff Taggart with growth and self-knowledge and John Fisher with people's health and well-being. Jonathan Long says '"spiritual" hints at all that is most sublime and profound about the human condition. It enshrines all that is most enduring and vital about the human self' (p. 49).

A Broad Spirituality

Hay, writing with Rebecca Nye, argues that, although spirituality is difficult to define, the various uses of the word could be plotted on a sliding scale. At one end of such a scale spirituality would mean 'a delicacy of awareness' such as 'a musical or poetic sensitivity.' At the other end of the scale would be 'mystical experience' in which a person discovers 'their oneness with the rest of reality or, if they are religiously devout … aspire to or have achieved mystical union with the Godhead' (1996, p. 7). They conclude:

> In spite of the extreme divergence, there is a degree of common ground between the ends of this continuum, for both refer to heightened awareness or attentiveness. We conjecture that spirituality in general is concerned with an awareness of and reflection upon the self and an holistic awareness of all that is not the self. (ibid)

This description of spirituality demonstrates a breadth of conceptual meaning important to many educationalists (and indeed to OFSTED). As said above, it is the breadth of meaning that often allows its inclusiveness, a pragmatic necessity for state schools. Breadth of meaning enables flexibility. The term 'spirituality' can be stretched to encompass a broad area well beyond the religious. So, while Martin Ashley uses language which at least grounds spirituality in the religious zone:

> The spiritually developed person is able to perceive meaning and purpose in life, as well as a mission or sense of purposeful vocation. He or she feels that all life is sacred and experiences feelings of wonder and awe which allow the perception of life as 'holy' (whether or not this is conceived in a religious sense). (p. 141)

Jane Mallick and Mike Watts, writing about drugs education, push its compass well beyond any such limits:

> Unsurprisingly, we have failed to develop any one single definition of spirituality [...] We are less interested in—say—formal religious definitions, than more general understandings of the word, such as: 'a sense of meaning of life', 'life satisfaction', 'wellbeing' or 'self-actualization'. [...] This is the sense in which we have chosen to conceptualize spirituality: people's attempts to make meaning of circumstances and situations, not simply through an appreciation of the immediate conditions, observable attitudes or palpable experiences that apply, but through reflective, sensitive, ethereal and transcendental means. It is a willingness to look continuously for meaning and purpose in life. (pp. 71–72)

And Terence McLaughlin, writing about sex education, seems to say it all:

> This domain involves a wide range of kinds of human sensitivity, experience, belief, judgement, response, disposition, motivation, commitment,virtue and achievement which is often related to a wide range of perspectives on broader matters such as the nature of reality, of persons and of the good.... [A] useful broad distinction for the purposes of the present discussion can be drawn between conceptions of 'spirituality' which are linked to, and housed within, a religious faith and tradition, on the one hand, and those which are more wide ranging in their focus and location, on the other hand. These can be described as 'religiously tethered' and 'religiously untethered' conceptions of 'spirituality' respectively. (pp. 224–225)

Whispers of Angels

But spirituality emerged from the depths of religion, and that drawing away was sometimes hard to do. Several authors, while they implied spirituality was broader than religion, used language retaining a strong religious flavour. For instance, Glenys Woods, Maggie O'Neill and Philip Woods write of the reality of 'the spiritual world' and of people 'consisting of body, soul and spirit' (p. 27). Newby calls for the introduction of 'ecstatic values' to schools which have a 'saving power' in a society which is 'lost' and in 'decay' (p. 44). Mark Chater, though generally seeming to divorce himself from religion, often uses colourful religious language: 'spirituality is seen as a third way, a crucified way ... it is the blood-soaked ground' (1998, p. 156).

Voices of Discord

There are those who strongly oppose the broad sweep approach to spirituality. In the IJCS those voices are heard through Andrew Wright and Michael Shire, although other authors make similar points elsewhere (see, for instance, Thatcher, 1999). Shire, writing from a religious perspective, criticises the 'universalist approach to the nature of spirituality':

> Such an universalist and syncretistic approach blurs the significant differences between religious traditions and often assumes a Western Rationalist position. (p. 53)

Andrew Wright's critique encompasses more than religious objections and is discussed below. John Hull places his discussion of spirituality and morality firmly within the context of religion and Christianity.

Although there is some disagreement with the inclusivity and breadth of spirituality, IJCS authors would generally agree with John Pridmore: 'To nurture the spirit of the child we may well talk about God but we do not have to' (p. 33).

Locating Spiritual Development in the Curriculum

Having said that, the early discussion of spiritual development in IJCS was chiefly located within the context of Religious Education. Spirituality's inclusiveness was intended to include all pupils—religious and secular—in RE lessons. Gradually, however, the discussion moved further a field into the broader curriculum.

Religious Education

Much of the discussion of spirituality in Religious Education focused on the value of affective or experiential approaches as opposed to cognitive approaches to spiritual development within RE. Many authors felt either that spiritual development must be affective and/or experiential rather than cognitive, or that the affective and/or experiential aspects were not given due emphasis. Authors' approaches took slightly different forms but they described a similar sense of unease.

The Affective or Experiential Approach to Spiritual Development Through RE

Jack Priestley argues that western rationality tends to make people sceptical about spirituality and unwilling to discuss it because it is deemed 'escapism from genuine, disciplined, rational thought' (p. 25).

> If the notion of the spiritual does not fit within the world of rational discourse which surrounds educational studies there are two possibilities. Either it has no substance and should be ignored or there is something wrong or inadequate about what for us constitutes rationality. (ibid)

Hay and Nye explain, 'Spirituality is not in the first place about knowledge, though it is about a "knowing" that becomes the subject of the process of cognitive development' (Hay & Nye, 1996, p. 8):

> Spiritual awareness cannot be taught, since like all awareness it is a biologically inbuilt constituent of what it is to be human. What the teacher can do is to help children to become 'aware of their awareness' and to reflect on this experience in the light of the culture within which it emerges. (Hay, 1997, p. 13–14)

Spirituality is essentially experiential, so RE should encourage awareness of the spiritual experience rather than emphasise the religious or cultural forms of spirituality. Like Hay, Glenys Woods uses evidence from the Alister Hardy research centre of the high incidence in contemporary society of transcendent spiritual experiences which she feels should inform educational policy so this area of human experience is included in the curriculum (Woods, 1996).

The Cognitive Approach to Spiritual Development Through RE

Andrew Wright, a forceful critic of the affective and experiential approaches to spiritual development through RE, 'attempts to deconstruct the working neutrality of spiritual education' (p. 8) as it emerges from the kind of approach discussed so far in this article. An authentic spiritual education, he says, requires spirituality be taught contextualised in religious tradition rather than in a disengaged experientialism. Religious Education should encourage children to think critically, giving them the linguistic tools necessary for spiritual development.

> In a national education system that places spiritual development at the centre of its educational aims, it is necessary to ground spiritual education in the nation's historical traditions, to understand spirituality in terms of national identity. [...] [T]he recognition that national identity is itself made up of a variety of spiritual traditions, not all of which sit easily with one another. [...] An authentic spiritual education must begin by recognising and nurturing children into the specific spiritual tradition they bring with them to the classroom, the spiritual outlook they already own. [...] Pupils will need to acknowledge and articulate their own spiritual tradition(s), and to be aided in moving towards increasingly appropriate forms of participation in them. (pp. 16–17)

Balancing Affective with Cognitive

There has been some vociferous debate over the affective cognitive divide, both in IJCS and elsewhere, with key players on both sides. So it was interesting that the overall analysis of the IJCS articles showed a majority of its authors favoured a balance of the two.

Shellie Levine argues cognitive spirituality should be balanced with experiential, or lived, spirituality.

> In order to delineate the cognitive underpinnings of spirituality it is crucial to explore the phenomenology of those actions, affects and ideations which are described by practitioners as lived spiritual experience. The abstractness of philosophical concepts invites correction by lived reality. (p. 129)

Similarly, David Torevell feels it is crucial for RE. to involve emotion and symbolism to enable cognitive understanding:

> 'Getting the feel' of a religion [...] is only possible by giving attention to embodied experiences of the sacred. [...] [A]ny cognitive grasp of doctrinal and philosophical teaching can only be fully appreciated if students are educated into the sorts of emotions to which those teachings bear witness. Religion cannot be understood without appreciating those emotions, which exist in relation to objects worthy of worship and awe. (p. 35)

Berryman describes spirituality as a 'general potential' but acknowledges 'spirituality needs the language of a specific religious tradition to be communicated because we do not learn any means of communication "in general" (p. 15). Spirituality, or 'knowing through contemplation,' should be encouraged through special experiential methodologies involving flow and play. So, while the language of a specific religious tradition is essential to the actualization and communication of spirituality, schools need to take care they do not destroy the inherent spirituality of children when they come to teach this.

Taggart argues for experiential learning and inwardness as ways to spiritual development and criticises OFSTED for placing undue emphasis on the *discussion* of spiritual *knowledge* rather than on *experience* of, for instance, 'stillness and contemplation' (1997, p. 36). However, he says, an exclusive emphasis on the affective is inappropriate. What is needed is 'a unified epistemology which incorporates feeling and imagination as well as logic and discursive reason' (2001, p. 327).

Beyond Religious Education and Toward Citizenship

Only recently have articles appeared in IJCS linking spirituality directly with subjects in the curriculum other than RE, and these were few in number. Pridmore looks to the literature of fairy tale and fantasy for spiritual opportunities, and Graham Rossiter's articles advocate the use of film and television. Pike's first article in IJCS illustrates how English lessons can play a major role in spiritual development through the use of poetry. His second looks at art lessons. Ashley relates spiritual development to environmental education. Terence McLaughlin explores the spiritual dimension of sex education. Mallick and Watts find spirituality in drugs education.

Where spiritual development really took off into the broad curriculum was in its application to personal growth and moral development. This was a significant leap because it took spirituality into the territory to be occupied by citizenship.

Spirituality and the Freedom to Grow

Each of the authors referred to in the last section above, put weight on spiritual development as development for personal growth. But *many* of the articles in the IJCS made this connection, and then made a further link with *freedom* for growth. This, in turn, involved much discussion of the need for a freeing up of teaching 'methods'. It also involved a critique of the current state of education in this country.

Before we go there, here are some examples of the discussion of spirituality as freedom for personal growth.

Taggart says spiritual education involves a process of growth and self-knowledge not unlike the psychotherapeutic approach of Carl Rogers.

> Rogers [...] maintains that people instinctively orient themselves towards growth and self-knowledge and that all that is required, in both therapy and education, is the provision of an environment that will facilitate this. (2001, p. 329)

Chater also equates spiritual development with a kind of therapy.

> Spiritual education, at its best, fosters growth and helps the individual to search for meaning. These processes are by no means painless for the learner: either by ignoring the search, or by engaging in it, s/he may experience frustration, loss, confusion, sadness, anger. The argument will be that we can summarize these painful experiences and name them as woundedness. [...] [W]e can see woundedness as a fundamental characteristic of all learners, by virtue of their humanity, but especially children. The child, as a learning spirit, can be understood to be wounded; the process of spiritual education can be understood therapeutically, knowledge can be understood as self-recovery. In this understanding, spiritual education is not therapy in itself, but can be metaphorically understood as such, and can have some therapeutic effects. (Chater, 1998, p. 147)

In a different article, Chater equates spirituality with struggle, arguing spiritual education is a process of struggle, a process enabling children to become whole and liberated, and survive (Chater, 2000). Sheryl Kujawa-Holbrook's article equates spiritual development specifically with girls' struggle for personal growth:

> [G]irls share a need to own their 'voice' and may struggle with issues of self-esteem and independence. The ethic of care shared by many girls suggests a latent sense of social responsibility that needs to be both shaped and challenged [...] [and] the need to develop more assertive behaviour on a variety of levels— spiritual, personal, social, and intellectual. (p. 304)

The need for growth translated for many authors into a need for a freeing up of approaches to teaching. Erricker says teachers should listen to children's narratives and must not impose views on children: 'children's understanding before adult authority, narrative before instruction' (p. 62). They should 'engage with the process of spiritual development rather than being concerned with a pre-determined outcome aligned to either moral ends or faith commitment' (p. 51). Pike calls for teaching methods involving a freer engagement with text. Fisher argues for a freeing up of teaching methods to enable 'teachers to be inspirational, getting students to question their philosophy of life' and allowing 'freedom of choice by the students, from responsible alternatives' (p. 47). Bosacki says children need to be enabled to develop emotionally and intellectually to find their own 'spiritual voice' and should not be directed.

> Our ultimate goal as humanistic, constructivist educators is not to produce non-feeling, direction-following experts, but to encourage children to develop a direction and voice of their own, which in turn will assist in the growth of the love of learning and the need to constantly search for meaning. (p. 119)

The focus on personal growth stemmed from a similar conceptual interest as the affective and experiential approaches to Religious Education, in other words with the (inner) self. However, the IJCS articles also demonstrated a long standing but increasing concern with the self *in relationship*, or 'relational consciousness'. So, the second route spirituality took into the broader curriculum was through its link with moral development.

Spirituality and the Freedom to be Moral

> Spiritual development, in the final instance is to do with recognising a consciousness which is shared. [...] Spiritual development starts with inner experience ('awareness—sensing'), and there is nothing world-denying about enlivening our imaginations and awareness so that we recognise our interdependence with it. Yet, as I have argued, schools are communities and experiential work needs to be undertaken with regard to the myths and archetypes of commonly appreciated culture ('value-sensing'). (Taggart, 1997, p. 43)

Taggart's account of the link between spirituality and morality was repeated in the ideas of many of the authors in the IJCS. The kind of freedom that develops personal or inner awareness leads to a feeling of relationship and an awareness of community. This is not about freedom of and for the individual.

> [I]ndividual self-sufficiency and personal freedom cannot be absolute values. Freedom means freedom for individual empowerment within various forms of community, social and global. (2001, p. 333)

Taggart, importantly along with Priestley, specifically says spirituality is *a-moral*, but this was not a widely shared view. For many IJCS authors spirituality was inherently moral and they wanted to show how the spiritual way to morality was preferable to a form of moral development that tried to impose moral rules. It was about a moral sensitivity, increasingly referred to in Hay and Nye's terms as 'relational consciousness', which did not need to be regimented by rules and codes of conduct but flowed naturally and freely in those who were more spirituality developed.

So Ashley calls for schools to promote 'transformative spiritual values' or 'a communitarian spirituality' (p. 131) rooted in 'relational consciousness', rather than the inculcation of moral, or civic, duty:

> [I]t is possible to identify a 'spiritual' view in which [...] pro-environmental behaviour would result, not from a sense of duty or obligation subject to weakness of will, but from a sense of personal vision, vocation or fulfilment. (p. 134)

Kay says spirituality leads to morality because it is to do with sensitivity to transcendence *and* relationship:

> The person who is spiritual, by this understanding, is someone who apprehends the transcendent and demonstrates this apprehension by a wider and more embracing cognitive perspective and a gentler and more reflective character. (p. 18)

Kane says spirituality leads to morality because spirituality is about love:

> When teachers open the world to children and children to the world and loving encounter, the children are nourished inwardly so that they may grow. With each lesson such children are not only informed but educated—given the sustenance necessary to Become. They will learn to transcend self-interest in deference to the wonder of which they are part, to receive the world with gratitude and to act with a sense of responsibility beyond self-interest. [...] [L]ove can help us educate children so that they have the courage, the strength and the wisdom to receive the gifts they are given and to grapple with the great tasks of their lives. (p. 7)

Ploeger says spirituality is 'a longing (which) never finds rest, for it sees the other in 'grief and longing [...] and urges a search for justice' (p. 16). Pike says spirituality is reflexive:

> Spirituality is central to education because it engenders such 'reflexiveness'. [...] The value of developing spiritual awareness lies, partly, in the vantage point it gives children from which they can interpret their own experiences and those of others. (2002, p. 19)

Stern makes the interesting point that, since a school represents the wider community it can function as the vehicle to enable the child to extend beyond the family to society as a whole: 'Schools are therefore centrally concerned with 'spirituality'— with 'real people' working in 'communities'' (p. 30).

Subversive Spirituality

If spirituality in schools is about encouraging moral sensitivity, relationship and community along with personal growth, it should sit well with citizenship education. However, there was another side to spirituality which emerged fairly consistently from the IJCS, sometimes stridently, sometimes more quietly, which may make spirituality and citizenship uneasy compatriots. This said, spirituality in schools is about allowing freedom for children's personal growth, enabling the creative thinking and relational feeling necessary for the development of morality and a sense of community. However, schooling, because it is influenced by western socio-economic values, inhibits this growth, thus inhibits moral development, and in turn threatens society. While only a few key players gave strong voice to this argument, many IJCS authors quietly echoed these concerns. Overall, it was a formidable chorus.

Several authors warned schooling can destroy children's spirituality. For instance, Newby says:

> Spiritual development through education may force us to focus upon ensuring that something is not lost that seems, all too often, to be lost through schooling. For the wonder of the child, its uninhibited curiosity, its sense of the being of creatures and its intercourse with the cosmos, is not to be ignored. (p. 48)

Hay and Nye warn spirituality can be eroded by contemporary, western culture, especially during schooling, and this could have a major negative social impact.

> One of the most important research findings about spiritual experience is its association with ethics [...] Almost without exception adults questioned about the influence of their spiritual insight say that it motivates an increased desire to care for those closest to them, to take issues of social justice more seriously and to be concerned about the total environment. [...] The importance of the built-in spirituality of the individual is that it is intrinsic. Spirituality cannot be taught. It can be and is very often crushed out of awareness during education. We urgently need to understand more about the processes that produce spiritual damage, so that they can be countered adequately, particularly in the school classroom. [...] [C]ultural change can be at odds with the requirements of biology, creating pathological consequences. Could the treatment of spirituality in contemporary Western culture be an illustration, particularly in the way it is handled with children? (Hay & Nye, 1996, pp. 13–14)

A number of authors referred to the de-valuing of education through an over emphasis on economic and utilitarian aims and ends. Kay says schools' recent emphasis on economic values cannot enhance children's spiritual growth. Clouder observes state education is driven, as it often has been historically, by economic and nationalistic considerations.

> The 'market solution' is proving to have a great attraction for politicians all over the world. The market is seen as a mechanism that can produce its own rules and has the added convenience of removing direct responsibility from the individuals themselves. [...] Self-interest and competition are assumed to be the keys to human nature and everyone is understood to be driven to work by these basic human instincts. What was previously preserved as a secret garden is now given the attributes of a pressurised market place. (p. 45)

Along with Pike, Clouder is critical of the utilitarian approach to education in the state sector and Newby argues the current educational philosophy, as enshrined in the National Curriculum approach, represents a threat because of its emphasis on economic values and political aims.

> I am arguing that our love of the world, as understood here, is under threat from a centrally-enforced, highly systematic, and instrumentally-justified curriculum, and that the solution lies, not in the return to a free-for-all in deciding the nature of the school curriculum, but in taking seriously the need for a deeper understanding of the nature of human well-being as the supreme aim of education. This can then enable us to temper the realistic, if pragmatic, demands made by the present socio-economic system upon schooling with an awareness of the need to allow the development of 'ecstatic' values. For, without such values, the individual has lost hope of finding an inner self. (p. 44)

He goes on to say the present socio-economic value system 'is destructive because it threatens the present and the future of the world' (ibid).

Hay refers to the fear of 'anarchy resulting from spiritual deafness,' to a concern about 'social decay' (Hay, 1997, p. 6) and, most recently, to contemporary western society forgetting relational consciousness because of its emphasis on individualism. To restore relational consciousness, spiritual education must be *subversive*.

> This way of conceiving of the tasks of spiritual education is to see them as twofold: simultaneously nurturing a natural predisposition and deconstructing a socially constructed individualism which is destructive of human community. The latter could be seen as a process of de-indoctrination, and from this perspective spiritual education has a subversive quality. (Hay, 2000, p. 47)

Woods *et al.* conclude state schools would need to be radically reformed if spiritual education was to have any hope of happening:

> [A] spiritually-centred education clashes with a detailed, closely prescribed curriculum driven predominantly by utilitarian, goal-orientated and economic considerations. (p. 37)

Paul Yates, in a complex argument, agrees with this bleak assessment. Yates examines in detail the cultural sources of neo-conservative political policy, and the end of liberalism and its replacement with rationalism. He portrays schools as modernist, bureaucratic institutions and concludes they are unable to accommodate the spiritual dimension because of the low professional status of teachers and their lack of involvement in curriculum development.

Hull concludes frighteningly:

> Elsewhere, I have discussed the ambiguity of spiritual values [...] In the present essay I have clarified this ambiguity by distinguishing between the life-enhancing values of healthy and carefully managed competition from the life-destroying values of ruthless and unjust competition. [...] I have traced the latter back into the destructive values which cascade down from the way that money is organized today [...] the greed and selfishness which that system inevitably promotes is the source of the culture of self-seeking which is so prominent in the spiritual lives of children and young people from advantaged homes, while it takes the form of apathy and defiance in the lives of disadvantaged young people. (p. 273)

And Priestly depressingly: 'We have lost our dreams and with that loss a young generation has nothing to strive for' (pp. 30–31).

Concluding Observations: is citizenship prepared for spirituality?

Much of the early debate about spiritual development stemmed from and took place within the curriculum context of Religious Education, but this article has tried to show that over time it spread well beyond this, seeing spirituality as having a particularly important role in personal, moral and social development. The spirituality which finally emerged from the IJCS looked something like this.

Spirituality is about space in the curriculum and an attentiveness in schools as a whole to the child as a person in need of space to grow and develop, who needs positive encouragement and help in this and who should be listened to and not given too much adult direction. This care will reap rewards in the form of an increased confidence and strength of character in young people and an increased awareness of their relationship with other people, with the environment, with communities and society, and with the world as a whole.

This all fits very well with the aims of citizenship.

However, much of the discussion of spiritual development was based in radical politics and philosophy. A number of authors were concerned with what they perceived to be the damaging effects of economic materialism on schooling. They sometimes claimed the educational reforms initiated by the 1988 and 1992 Education Acts, and particularly the National Curriculum, demonstrated an unbalanced concern with economic and utilitarian aims. This they saw as resulting in, for instance, an over emphasis on cognitive learning and content knowledge, an erosion of the status and energy of teachers, and an emphasis on school as a competitive market where the child is unable to flourish and grow as a person. A number of authors claimed western society is in decay, and that unless attention is paid to this problem in schools, social and community cohesion will be undermined.

Such a radical spirituality within citizenship would be challenging.

Mary Earl and Liam Gearon suggest we guard against simplistic and na¨ive constructions of what we mean by spirituality. Earl explores the shadow side of human spirituality, problematising the naively positive understandings of spirituality given by some educationalists and particularly by government which is 'concerned with awe, wonder and mystery but not with the difficulties of holding these together with degradation, despair and destructiveness' (p. 277). Gearon goes even further. He calls for a 'spirituality of dissent'.

> A spirituality of dissent resists easy assimilation into the systems of cultural representation—locally, nationally and globally—and always presents a challenge to the systems which control such representation. […] [W]ar, poverty and starvation all mock the prevalence of self-indulgent models of cultural and spiritual development, as for instance, in the glib reiteration of 'awe and wonder' in Western educational contexts. (pp. 296–297)

Gearon's words are shocking and disturbing. But I hope this article has demonstrated that Gearon does not represent a lone voice.

Spirituality within citizenship could be dynamite.

References

Ashley, M. (2000) Behaviour change and environmental citizenship: a case for spiritual development, *International Journal of Children's Spirituality*, 5(2), pp. 131–145.

Berryman, J. W. (1997) Spirituality, religious education and the dormouse, *The International Journal of Children's Spirituality*, 2(1), pp. 9–22.

Bosacki, S. L. (1998) Is silence really golden? The role of spiritual voice in folk pedagogy and folk psychology, *International Journal of Children's Spirituality*, 3(2), pp. 109–121.

Chater, M. (1998) Woundedness and the learning child-spirit—ontology and epistemology of a therapeutic education, *International Journal of Children's Spirituality*, 3(2), pp. 147–157.

Chater, M. (2000) Spirituality as struggle: poetics, experience and the place of the spiritual in educational encounter, *International Journal of Children's Spirituality*, 5(2), pp. 193–201.

Clouder, C. (1998) The spiritual dimension and autonomy, *International Journal of Children's Spirituality*, 3(1), pp. 43–49.

Copley, T. (2000) *Spiritual Development in the State School* (Exeter, University of Exeter Press). DFEE & QCA (1999) *National Curriculum Handbooks for Secondary Teachers* (London, QCA Publications).

Earl, M. (2001) Shadow and spirituality, *International Journal of Children's Spirituality*, 6(3), pp. 277–288.

Erricker, C. (1998) Spiritual confusion: a critique of current educational policy in England and Wales, *International Journal of Children's Spirituality*, 3(1), pp. 51–63.

Erricker, C. & Erricker, J. (2000) *Reconstructing Religious, Spiritual and Moral Education* (London, RoutledgeFalmer).

Fisher, J. W. (1999) Helps to fostering students' spiritual health, *International Journal of Children's Spirituality*, 4(1), pp. 29–49.

Gearon, L. (2001) A spirituality of dissent: religion, culture and post-colonial criticism, *International Journal of Children's Spirituality*, 6(3), pp. 289–298.

Hay, D. (1997) Spiritual education and values, *International Journal of Children's Spirituality*, 2(2), pp. 5–16.

Hay, D. (2000) Spirituality versus individualism: why we should nurture relational consciousness, *International Journal of Children's Spirituality*, 5(1), pp. 37–48.

Hay, D. & Nye, R. (1996) Investigating children's spirituality: the need for a fruitful hypothesis, *International Journal of Children's Spirituality*, 1(1), pp. 6–16.

Hull, J. M. (2001) Competition and spiritual development, *International Journal of Children's Spirituality*, 6(3), pp. 263–275.

Jackson, R. (2003) *International Perspectives on Citizenship, Education and Religious Diversity*, (London, RoutledgeFalmer).

Kane, J. (1997) Love as educational reality, *International Journal of Children's Spirituality*, 1(2), pp. 5–7.

Kay, W. (1996) Fowler, spirituality and values in church schools, *International Journal of Children's Spirituality*, 1(1), pp. 17–22.

Kujawa-Holbrook, S. A. (2001) Courage and resistance: spiritual formation and mentoring girls for religious leadership, *International Journal of Children's Spirituality*, 6(3), pp. 299–310.

Levine, S. (1999) Children's cognition as the foundation of spirituality, *International Journal of Children's Spirituality*, 4(2), pp. 121–140.

Long, J. (2000) Spirituality and the idea of transcendence, *International Journal of Children's Spirituality*, 5(2), pp. 147–161.

Mallick, J. & Watts, M. (2001) Spirituality and drugs education: a study in parent/child communication, *International Journal of Children's Spirituality*, 6(1), pp. 67–83.

Mclaughlin, T. H. (2001) A spiritual dimension to sex education?, *International Journal of Children's Spirituality*, 6(2), pp. 223–232.

Newby, M. (1996) Spiritual development and love of the world, *International Journal of Children's Spirituality*, 1(1), pp. 44–51.

Pike, M. A. (2000) Spirituality, morality and poetry, *International Journal of Children's Spirituality*, 5, p. 2.

Pike, M. A. (2002) Aesthetic distance and the spiritual journey: educating for spiritually and morally significant experiences across the art and literature curriculum, *International Journal of Children's Spirituality*, 7(1), pp. 9–21.

Ploeger, A. (1997) Longing: the spiritual source of religion, explained in a Christian context, *International Journal of Children's Spirituality*, 2(2), pp. 17–24.

Pridmore, J. (2002) Talking of God and talking of fairies: discourses of spiritual development in the works of George MacDonald and in the curriculum, *International Journal of Children's Spirituality*, 7(1), pp. 23–35.

Priestley, J. (1997) Spirituality, curriculum and education, *International Journal of Children's Spirituality*, 2(1), pp. 23–34.

Rossiter, G. (1996) Science, film and television: an introductory study of the 'alternative' religious stories that shape the spirituality of children and adolescents, *International Journal of Children's Spirituality*, 1(1), pp. 52–67.

Rossiter, G. (1997) The shaping influence of film and television on young people's spirituality: implications for moral and religious education, part 2, *International Journal of Children's Spirituality*, 1(2), pp. 21–35.

Rossiter, G. (1999) The shaping influence of film and television on the spirituality and identity of children and adolescents: an educational response, part 3, *International Journal of Children's Spirituality*, 4(2), pp. 207–224.

Shire, M. J. (1997) Jewish spiritual development and curriculum theory, *International Journal of Children's Spirituality*, 2(2), pp. 53–59.

Stern, J. (2001) John Macmurray, spirituality, community and real schools, *International Journal of Children's Spirituality*, 6(1), pp. 25–39.

Taggart, G. (1997) Spirituality and post-modernism: a classroom perspective, *International Journal of Children's Spirituality*, 2(1), pp. 35–45.

Taggart, G. (2001) Nurturing spirituality: a rationale for holistic education, *International Journal of Children's Spirituality*, 6(3), pp. 325–339.

Thatcher, A. (1999) *Spirituality and the Curriculum*, (London, Cassell).

Torevell, D. (2000) Acting out of affections: embodiment, morality and (post) modernity, *International Journal of Children's Spirituality*, 5(1), pp. 27–36.

Watson, J. (2000) OFSTED's spiritual dimension: an analytical audit of inspection reports, *Cambridge Journal of Education*, 31(2), pp. 205–219.

Watson, J. (2003) *Citizenship Education and its Impact on Religious Education*, Farmington Report, Farmington Institute for Christian Studies website: *www.farmington.ac.uk/documents/reports*. WOODS, G. (1996) Poor relation or honoured guest? The place of the transcendent in a state education system that seeks to promote spiritual development, *International Journal of Children's Spirituality*, 1(1), pp. 31–43.

Woods, G., O'neill, M. & Woods, P. A. (1997) Spiritual values in education: lessons from Steiner? *International Journal of Children's Spirituality*, 2(2), pp. 25–40.

Wright, A. (1997) Embodied spirituality: the place of culture and tradition in contemporary educational discourse on spirituality, *International Journal of Children's Spirituality*, 1(2), pp. 8–20.

Yates, P. (1999) The bureaucratization of spirituality, *International Journal of Children's Spirituality*, 4(2), pp. 179–193.

Helps to fostering students' spiritual health

John W. Fisher

ABSTRACT
Interviews with 98 teachers from a variety of schools were used to develop a definition of spiritual health, and to establish how these teachers thought spiritual health might best be fostered and what hindered its development in the school curriculum. A recurring theme, which seemed to be coming through the comments from teachers in this study, was the very important role that teachers play in helping students develop relationships. This was of vital importance as spiritual health was seen as being reflected in the quality of relationships that students develop with themselves, others, the environment, and with a Transcendent Other. The characteristics of teachers most frequently mentioned as desirable for the promotion of spiritual health were classified as follows

- *caring, sensitive, personal approach;*
- *concern for individuals;*
- *committed to personal beliefs and values.*

Investigation of these teacher characteristics showed variation by gender, personal view of spiritual health, major curriculum concern, teacher and school type. Implications of these variations are discussed in this paper, together with the role of Spiritual Facilitator, to help nurture students' spiritual health.

Introduction

Mention of students' spiritual well-being was first made in Australian and Victorian state curriculum documents in 1994. It is also contained in *Australia's Common and Agreed Goals for Schooling in the Twenty-first Century* (MCEETYA, 1998). This begs the question, 'what is spiritual well-being?' According to Bensley:

> recently a paradigm shift has been occurring in health education and health promotion practices. The increased emphasis on the spiritual dimension of health... has begun to shift the focus of health education/promotion efforts from negative health outcomes to increasing positive quality of life. (1996, p. 390)

'Spirituality formed the heart of the holistic health movement of the seventies. It was viewed as the umbrella of health components, affecting every area of the person' (Goodloe & Arreola, 1992, p. 223). Even though there is a clear separation oi Church and State in America, the concepts of spirituality and spiritual health have been a pressing concern of the health disciplines there, since 1979. While many health professionals seek to study and implement spiritual health concepts (Osman & Russell, 1979; Chapman, 1986; Jose, 1987;

Bellingham *et al.*, 1989; Bensley, 1991; Seaward, 1991; Goodloe & Arreola, 1992; Hawks *et al.*, 1995), others are still skeptical and find spiritual issues problematic (Fahlberg & Fahlberg, 1991).

'That there is as yet no consensus of definition of spirituality or of spiritual health... should be seen as part of the normal evolution of any new and emerging area of study, and not a fatal deficiency' (Diaz, 1993, pp. 324–325). Health educators in the USA, who support the spiritual dimension to health, state that this concept can be taught effectively (Banks *et al.*, 1984, p. 17).

Spiritual health could well be called the forgotten factor in health promotion in Australia, paralleling the situation which existed in the USA in the mid-1980s (Chapman, 1986, p. 38). The editors of the Supplement to the *Journal of Paediatrics and Child Health* in 1993 raised the issue that there is an 'urgent need to set a new agenda for adolescent health in Australia in the 1990s', as many of the serious risks to health, such as drug use, violence, stress, depression and suicide, are experienced earlier in life than in the past (Bennett & Nutbeam, 1993, SI). In the same journal, Resnick *et al.* (1993, S3) reported an American study which concluded that a sense of religious/spiritual connectedness functioned as a protective factor against highrisk behaviours for adolescents, ranked in importance after 'school', and 'family connectedness'.

It can be argued that if schools can enhance spiritual connectedness, they will be playing a greater role in enhancing the total well-being of their students. This paper contains a brief overview of aspects of connectedness as we look at the nature of spiritual health, together with detailed analysis as to what a variety of teachers believe helps and hinders its development in schools.

Nature of Spiritual Health

One of the earliest attempts at a definition of spiritual health or well-being was that proposed by the National Interfaith Coalition on Aging (1975), which suggested that 'spiritual well-being is the affirmation of life in a relationship with *God, self, community,* and *environment* that nurtures and celebrates wholeness' (from Ellison, 1983, p. 331) [my emphasis]. From an analysis of recent literature, it was shown that these four sets of relationships are variously mentioned in discussions of spirituality, spirituality and health, and spiritual health (Fisher, 1998, p. 24). The four relationships are of a person with:

- self
- others
- environment
- something/some-One beyond the human level (Transcendent Other).

My initial definition of spiritual health, based on these four sets of relationships, was refined, after analysing the teachers' input, to become:

> Spiritual health is a fundamental dimension of people's overall health and well-being, permeating and integrating all the other dimensions of health (i.e. the physical, mental, emotional, social and vocational).
>
> In addition, spiritual health is a dynamic state of being, shown by the extent to which people live in harmony within relationships in the following domains of spiritual well-being:

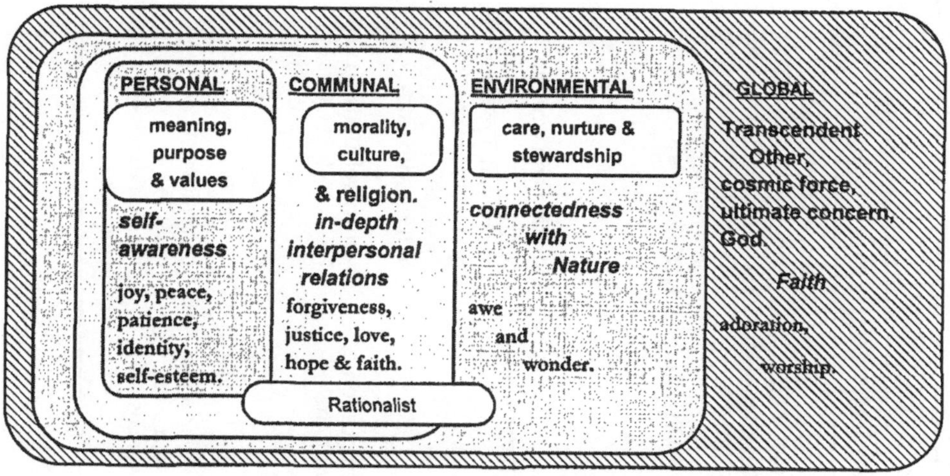

Figure 1. Spiritual Well-being-expressed by the quality of *relationships* in each DOMAIN.

- *Personal domain-wherein* one intra-relates with oneself with regards to meaning, purpose and values in life. The human spirit creates self-awareness, relating to self-esteem and identity.
- *Communal domain-as* expressed in the quality and depth of interpersonal relationships, between self and others, relating to morality, culture and religion. This includes love, justice, hope & faith in humanity.
- *Environmental domain-past* care and nurture for the physical and biological, to a sense of awe and wonder; for some, the notion of unity with the environment.
- *Global* domain-relationship of self with some-thing or some-One beyond the human level (i.e. ultimate concern; cosmic force; transcendent reality; or God). This involves faith toward, adoration and worship of, the source of Mystery of the universe.

It is important to note the dynamic nature of spiritual health. A person's state of being is generally not static; as s/he faces challenges, struggles to maintain harmony, develops character and builds up the four sets of relationships, so spiritual health improves. The quality of relationship in each domain constitutes a person's *spiritual well-being* in that domain. An individual's *spin"tual health,* their state of being, was seen to be indicated by the combined effect of spiritual well-being in each of the domains embraced by the individual. The four domains are not isolated, but are inter-related. Therefore, it was assumed that spiritual health was enhanced by developing positive relationships in each domain and increased by embracing more domains.

The notion of progressive synergism was proposed here to help explain the relationship between the domains. The Personal domain can be seen as a narrow base, in which a person trusts her- or him-self to be sufficient for the formation of her/his spiritual health. Few teachers expressed that view in my study. The Communal domain is seen to build on the Personal domain as well as building it up. In other words, the meaning, purpose and values developed *through self-awareness,* are precursors to, yet enhanced by, the development of morality, culture and religion through *in-depth inter-personal relationships.* Similarly, *connectedness with nature* should build on, and build up, self-awareness and

Table 1. A Model of Spiritual Well-being

	Domains of spiritual well-being			
	Personal	Communal	Environmental	Global
KNOWLEDGE ASPECT – filtered by world-view	meaning, purpose and values	morality, culture, and religion	care, nurture and stewardship of the physical, eco political and social environment	transcendent Other – ultimate concern Tillich – cosmic force New Age – God for Christians Jews and Moslems
INSPIRATIONAL ASPECT – *essence and* motivation – filtered by beliefs	– human spirit creates awareness – *self-consciousness*	– *in-depth interpersonal relations* – reaching the heart of humanity	*connectedness with* Nature/ Creation	***Faith***
EXPRESSED AS	– joy, fulfilment, – peace, patience, – freedom, – humility – identity, integrity – self-esteem	– love – forgiveness – justice – hope & faith in humanity – trust	– sense of awe and wonder – valuing Nature/Creation	adoration and worship being: – at one with Creator – of the essence of the universe – in tune with God
ASSESSED BY	attitude and demeanour individual behaviour, – participation – contentment – body language	– behaviour toward others – tolerance, service, – respect – contribution to commonwealth	extent of identification and unity with the environment	quality of relationship with Transcendent Other
DEVELOPED THROUGH	– encouragement – self-talk – teacher model – personal devpt	– relating to others – devotions – HG/PCare – religious values	communion with nature – awareness and awe – peak experiences	– commitment – nurture – meditation, prayer – worship

in-depth inter-personal relationships, with *Faith* embracing the other three relationships as well as being fostered by them. There was a fifth personal view of spiritual health, called Rationalist. The 9% of teachers in this study seen to be holding this view only embraced the knowledge aspects within the first three domains of spiritual well-being (illustrated by the clear box in Figure 1). They did not accept the transcendental/inspirational aspects of the relationships, which the literature indicated were necessary for complete spiritual well-being. As such, the Rationalists held a restricted view of spiritual well-being compared with the other teachers. In Figure 1, the knowledge aspects of each DOMAIN are written in bold type, at the top of each cell. The inspiration aspects of each DOMAIN are written in italics, in the centre of each cell. The expressions of well-being in each DOMAIN are written in roman type, at the bottom of each cell.

Table 1 is a summary of the initial model of spiritual well-being developed from the literature, enhanced by feedback from teachers in my study.

Of the 98 teachers in my study, the personal views of 97 of them were classified into one of five types of spiritual well-being. A full description of the Ideal Types was given in the paper presented at Roehampton in June last year (Fisher, 1997):

- *Personalists* embraced the Personal domain *as* spiritual well-being;
- *Communalists* embraced the Communal domain *as* spiritual well-being;
- *Environmentalists* embraced the Environmental domain *as* spiritual well-being;
- *Globalists* embraced the Global domain *as* spiritual well-being;
- *Rationalists* embraced the knowledge, not the inspirational aspects of the first three domains.

When the teachers' personal views of spiritual well-being were compared by school type in my study, more of the teachers in the State schools had views representative of Rationalists, Personalists and Communalists and markedly less as Globalists compared with the whole sample (see Table 2). This was not surprising considering half of the State school teachers expressed no religious affiliation. As would be expected, the Catholic and other Christian schools contained the greatest share of Globalists.

Table 2. Personal view of spiritual well-being by school type

Personal view of school well-being/ school type	*n*	Rationalist	Personalist	Communalist	Environmentalist	Globalist
State	20	**35%**	**15%**	**30%**	**15%**	**5%**
Catholic	19	*0%*	5%	*16%*	*0%*	79%
Other Christian	49	*4%*	*0%*	*10%*	*0%*	**86%**
Other non-govt	9	*0%*	*0%*	33%	**22%**	***44%***
Whole sample	97	9%	4%	18%	5%	64%

Note: bold Figures represent 10% variation from the whole sample response, italics represent <whole sample value.

Table 3. Quality of teaching factors perceived as important in promoting spiritual health

Teacher approach (53%)			Relation to others (51%)		Teacher model (43%)
encouraging	help students	acknowledge students	respect	forgiveness	teacher as role model
be positive	be available	listen to students	courtesy	tolerance	hidden curriculum
show love	respect students	challenge individuals	cooperation	caring	teacher presence
nurture	value students				

Helps For Promoting Spiritual Health

Using open-ended questions would not exhaustively cover the teachers' views on any topic. But it was hoped they would provide the factors considered most important to the teachers. The nature of the questions asked in the interviews helped fine tune teachers' views, or in fact, helped raise awareness of factors not previously thought of. For example, the place of environmental awareness in promoting spiritual health appeared to jump markedly in importance, when the teachers were asked about it specifically.

Details of Factors Perceived as Important in Promoting Spiritual Health

The first three factors (teacher approach, relation to others, teacher model) which were derived from the teachers' comments on promotion of spiritual health, re1ated to the quality of teaching in schools. When discussing ways of promoting spiritual health in schools, the teachers' positive, empathic approach to students was rated most highly (53% of the teachers raised an issue classified in this factor), followed closely by the development of relations with others (51%). The teacher as role model was mentioned by 43% of the teachers as important in developing spiritual health in students. Details of the teachers' responses, which were selected to make these three factors, are listed in Table 3.

These results compare favourably with the view of Hood Morris who stated that relationships for spiritual well-being are enhanced by 'kindness, gentleness, warmth, empathy and appreciation' (1996, p. 444).

The specific religious activities, featured in the top ten factors, would be most effectively undertaken by teachers with suiTable life experiences from which to encourage students in the development of these areas. In other words, it is difficult, if not impossible, to meaningfully teach what one does not know. It was not surprising that these religious factors were rated highly in this study because the sample of interviewees contained 77% of teachers from schools with religious ethos. Table 4 contains details of the responses included in each of the five religious factors.

Variations in Promoting Spiritual Health by Teachers' Personal Views of Spiritual Health

There appears to be a strong correlation between the teachers' personal views of spiritual health and ways in which they believed spiritual health of students could be promoted in

Table 4. Religious activities seen to *be* important in fostering spiritual health

Devotions (41%)	Religious values (34%)	Religious classes (32%)	Relation with God (30%)	Religious services (30%)
devotions retreats prayer	ethics morals religion	Religious Education Bible	worship love God	mass liturgy celebration
meditation ISCF*	culture faith	Scripture		Chapel

* Inter-School Christian Fellowship.

schools. The Rationalists and Personalists emphasized factors which can be influenced by people's thoughts and actions. They showed little support for, and in some cases opposition to, religious activities and relations with God, as ways of enhancing spiritual health. The Rationalists rated teacher model (+ 24%, indicating the variation of this sample from the group as a whole), discipline (+ 33%), personal development (+ 21%) higher than average, with religious classes (-21%), religious services (-30%), devotions (-41%) and relation with God (-63%) much lower than the whole sample. The Personalists showed increased interest in personal development (+ 27%), no support for religious values (-34%) and devotions (-41%), and opposition to relation with God (-55%). These results were consistent with the Rationalists' and Personalists' personal beliefs that humans arc the authors and perfecters of their own spiritual health.

The Communalists rated more highly than average the activities which require group cohesion-devotions (+ 12%), Home Group/Pastoral Care (+ 19%), and religious values (+ 13%), with no support for developing relations with God (-30%).

Environmental awe featured more strongly than average for the Environmentalists as a way to develop spiritual health. For Mr. Kidman, the Aboriginal students saw the environment 'like a library around them' strongly contributing a sense of awe and wonder, in the process of enhancing their spiritual health. The Environmentalists ignored devotions (-41%), religious classes (-32%) and services (-30%), and relations with God (-30%) as means to achieving this end.

The Globalists understandably had increased focus on devotions (+ **11**%), and relation with God (+ 12%) as important means by which to promote student spiritual health.

Table 5 shows the percentage of teachers, with the stated *personal views of spiritual health,* whose responses were classified into the key factors related to promotion of spiritual health.

Variations in Promoting Spiritual Health by School Type

For the teachers in State schools, the principles of developing relations with others (+ 14%) and discipline (+ 13%) featured more highly than across the whole sample. It was disappointing, but not surprising, to find lower than average concern for religious values (-14%) and religious classes (-22%), no support for devotions (-41%) or religious services (-30%), and opposition to relationship with God (-45%) by some of these State school teachers.

It seems the Catholic school teachers had high expectations of themselves with regard to creating supportive environments in which their students could develop spiritual health,

Table 5. Key factors relating teachers' personal views of spiritual health to its promotion

Rationalist ($n = 9$)		Personalist ($n = 4$)		Communalist ($n = 17$)		Environmentalist ($n = 5$)		Globalist ($n = 62$)	
teacher model	67	teacher approach	75	tr approach	53	env. awareness	40	tr approach	53
discipline	**55**	pers. development	50	devotions	53	env. awe	**40**	devotions	**52**
env. awareness	55	devotions	***0***	HG/PCare	47	devotions	***0***	relation to God	**42**
pers. development	44	religious values	***0***	religious values	47	religious classes	***0***	religious services	39
religious classes	*11*	relation to God	***–25***	relation to God	***0***	religious services	***0***	env. awareness	*31*
religious services	***0***					relation to God	***0***	pers. Development	*16*
devotions	***0***								
relation to God	***–33***								

Note: Bold Figures represent > 10% variation from whole sample value. Italics represent <whole sample value.

with increased emphasis on teacher approach (+ 31%), devotions (+ 22%), religious services (+ 28%), religious values (+ 8%) and teacher model (+ 15%).

For teachers in the other Christian schools, religious classes (+ 19%), devotions (+ 8%), relation with God (+ 13%) and self-talk (+ 9%) were mentioned more frequently as means of promoting student spiritual health, whereas teacher model (-8%), environmental awareness (-5%), religious values (-7%), and discipline (-10%) were not considered as important, very slightly lower than the whole sample response, illustrating that these teachers were more interested in relations than rules.

For the teachers in the other non-government schools, religious values (+55%) and discipline (+ 34%) featured strongly, especially for the staff in the Islamic and Jewish schools, for whom devotions (+ 15%) were also of importance in fostering spiritual health. Environmental awe (+ 22%) was considered to be of importance to the teachers in the Aboriginal and Waldorf schools. The connectedness of the Aboriginal people to their Mother Earth has previously been mentioned. For Mrs. Wadtke, the way the Waldorf school differed from other schools is in the curriculum, where 'you're not going to give a dead, cold, clinical view of the world. You'll give other, imaginative truths about animals and about plants and picture them as connected with the cosmos in an imaginative way'.

It was interesting to note that none of the teachers in the other non-government schools mentioned relation with God (-30%) as a means of fostering spiritual health of students in their schools. Religious classes (-21%) did not feature very highly either. Maybe the teachers in these schools considered that the students have enough already, so these areas do not need any more consideration.

Details of variations in promotion of spiritual health by school type are listed in Table 6. The Figures show the percentage of teachers of different school type whose comments were attributed to the listed factors, perceived as important in promoting spiritual health.

Valued Teacher Characteristics Perceived as Desirable for Promoting Spiritual Health

A recurring theme, which seemed to be coming through the comments from teachers in my study, was the very important role that teachers play in helping students develop relationships. This was of vital importance as spiritual well-being is seen as being reflected in the quality of relationships that students develop with themselves, others, the environment, and with a Transcendent Other.

The interviewees in this study were asked to list the key characteristics of a teacher whom they saw to be really good at promoting spiritual health. Ninety-two teachers responded positively to this question. Only one person, Ms. Ehrlich said she did not know a teacher who was good at promoting spiritual health, which she had described as related to religion, a topic not discussed in her State school.

As would be expected, the characteristics of teachers most frequently mentioned as desirable for the promotion of spiritual health were classified as follows:

- caring, sensitive, personal approach (70%);
- concern for individuals (68%);
- committed to personal beliefs and values (57%).

Table 6. School type and promotion of spiritual health

State (n = 20)		Catholic (n = 19)		Other Christian (n = 49)		Other non-government (n= 9)	
relation to others	**65**	teacher approach	**84**	Religious classes	**51**	religious values	**89**
env. awareness	45	devotions	**63**	devotions	49	discipline	**56**
discipline	**35**	religious services	**58**	relation to God	**43**	devotions	56
discussions	***20***	teacher model	**58**	self-talk	39	env. awareness	44
self-talk	***20***	religious values	42	teachermodel	*35*	env. awe	22
religious values	***20***	relation to others	**32**	env.awareness	*31*	religious classes	***11***
religious classes	***20***	religious classes	*26*	religious values	*27*	HG/PCare	***11***
devotions	***0***	relation to God	*26*	discipline	***12***	relation to God	***0***
relation to God	***–15***						

Note: Bold Figures represent > 10% variation from whole sample response, italics represent <whole sample value.

Table 7. Teacher characteristics perceived as being of prime importance in promoting spiritual health

Caring	Sensitive (70%)	Personal	Concern for individual (68%)	Personal beliefs/values (57%)
care help nurture love/compassion kids followed up living Gospel welfare	fair consistent flexible sensitive perceptive cries with students concern for souls prayerful not pretentious emotional	like people student interest teacher of children relate well people important receptive of others enjoy people rapport friendly personal	consideration understand difficulties seek out people self-esteem concern aware of needs relate to individual understand kids get alongside encourage build bridges give hope	confident in/ convinced of b. faithful to b. know heart life force within 'together' people, integrated passionate about b. know purpose Christian faith in service of God love the Lord believe religion fruit of Holy Spirit

Details of the responses selected to make these characteristics are listed in Table 7.

Westgate mentioned Weiss's (1974) six aspects of social support (caring, belonging, assisting, advising, evaluating, nurturing) as being desirable for support from a spiritual community (1996, p. 32). Each of these six aspects is included in the prime characteristics of teachers determined in my study (Table 7). In describing a pedagogy best suited to enhance spirituality, Goudzwaard said, 'Its characteristics can be summarised in the "three Ls" of listening, leading and loving' (1997, p. 47), the practical expressions of which are included in Table 7.

The first of the three teachers' characteristics, 'caring', was stated as being of prime importance in educating doctors (Wallace, 1997, p. 253) as 'the most important thing that [medical] educators can do as they bend to their task is to care'. The first two characteristics of good spiritual health promoters parallel an essential component of effective helping relationships in health education practice, derived from the literature by van Ryn and Heaney (1997, p. 683), that of 'providing unconditional acceptance and positive regard for clients'.

Ross reported 'that the most powerful factor determining how nurses gave spiritual care was their personal faith/value system' (1996, p. 42). This factor, 'personal beliefs/values', was considered to be of third highest importance in promoting spiritual health of students. Although teachers need to be authentic as far as their values and beliefs are concerned, they need to be wary not to impose these on their students. There is no such thing as values-free education. Teachers should be more than purveyors of knowledge. Forming a knowledge base about the four sets of relationships is important, but not sufficient, for promotion of spiritual health. If schools are places where students can learn about humanity and their place in it, should not teachers be able to inspire students to experience the depth of connectedness in each relationship, as appropriate to their school's ethos? A considered knowledge base could help students gain meaning from their experiences, and in schools there is generally the safety of numbers, with more than one adult to prevent enthusiastic excesses by zealots, who might attempt to overly influence students.

If students are not given the opportunity to consider issues of meaning, purpose, values, ethics, religion, and environment in the safety of school, they may fall foul of individual, charismatic leaders of obscure cults, which have led to past catastrophes such as Jonestown, Waco and the Heaven's Gate followers. However, anecdotes abound about well-intentioned religious leaders who turn off, rather than inspire, their congregations. The development of relationships (based on genuine love, care and commitment), rather than rules for living (based on legalism and conformity) should free students to reach their potential, thus optimizing their spiritual health. This concurs with a biblical principle 'the letter kills, but the Spirit gives life' (2 Cor. 3:6 NIV).

Variations in Valued Teacher Characteristics by Teacher Type

The Principals had a higher than average interest in the teachers' concern for the individual (+ 17%). As well as being concerned for the development of the individual (+ 16%), the Curriculum Coordinators were also more interested in staff being good teachers (+ 21%) and dedicated (+ 10%) to be most able to enhance the students' spiritual health.

It was surprising to see that the Welfare Coordinators had slightly lower expectations of the teachers being caring/sensitive/personal (-10%), as well as being good teachers (-27%). The Welfare Coordinators as a group had previously been shown to have greater humanitarian than religious concerns, so it was not surprising to find their lower interest in the teachers' personal beliefs (- 17%).

The Chaplains/RE Coordinators were true to form, with higher expectations of the teachers being caring/sensitive/personal (+ 10%), having strong personal beliefs (+ 16%), as well as greater confidence (+ 12%), and being personable (+ 27%), characteristics which would stand them in good stead for the development of relationships with people and God. As a group, they were less concerned with the focus on the individual (-25%), and the need to be a good teacher (-17%), than for the sample as a whole. Many religious groups talk of the religious community, or body of believers, so it is not unusual to find a lesser focus on the individuality of the student by the Chaplains/RE Coordinators.

Table 8 shows the percentages of teachers in each group who expressed concern about the stated characteristic being important for the promotion of spiritual health.

Variations in Valued Teacher Characteristics by School Type

The teachers in the State (+ 1 0%) and Catholic schools (+ 11%) expressed greater concern for individuals than the sample average, with teachers in the other Christian schools (- 14%) showing less. The other Christian school teachers would presumably show more concern for the corporate development of students as part of the body of Christ, rather than in individualism, which appears to be a feature of the current generation.

The Catholic school teachers expressed their concerns for the quality of teaching, with higher expectations of good teachers (+ 16%), who were dedicated (+ 10%).

The State school teachers were consistent with their limited desire for religious activities in their schools, by showing lesser concern about the teachers' beliefs/values (-40%) influencing the students' spiritual health, although values are not necessarily religious. In contrast to the State school teachers, those in the other Christian (+ 13%) and other non-government (+ 21 %) schools showed greater than average concern for the teachers'

Table 8. Teacher characteristics seen as important by different types of teachers

Teacher type/ characteristic	Whole sample	Principal ($n = 20$)	Curriculum Coordinator ($n = 19$)	Welfare Coordinator ($n = 10$)	Chaplain/RE Coordinator ($n = 15$)	Other teachers ($n = 28$)
caring/sensitive/ personal	70%	70	74	*60*	80	*64*
concern for individual	68%	85	84	70	***47***	*57*
beliefs/values	57%	*50*	63	***40***	**73**	*54*
confident	41%	*30*	47	*30*	**53**	43
good teacher	37%	40	58	*10*	*20*	39
dedicated	37%	*30*	47	*30*	40	39
communication	22%	*15*	26	*20*	27	25
personable	20%	***10***	21	*10*	**47**	*14*
calm	16%	*5*	16	30	*7*	25

Note: Figures represent percentage of that *teacher group* whose comments were attributed to the stated characteristic. Bold Figures represent > 10% variation from whole sample response, italics represent <whole sample value.

beliefs having an influence on the promotion of spiritual health. The latter viewpoint seems more reasonable, as a person's beliefs/values must influence their world-view, and the basis for forming relationships, thus their spiritual health.

Contrary opinions were also expressed about the personable nature of the teacher influencing spiritual health promotion. The other Christian school teachers (+ 12%) were more positively inclined to this view in contrast to the State school teachers who ignored it as a possibility (-20%) of having any influence in developing spiritual health.

The other non-government school teachers expressed greater concern about the confidence level (+ 15%), but less than average concern over the caring nature (-25%) and dedication (-26%) of their teachers in promoting spiritual health of students.

Table 9 contains details of the teacher characteristics considered of value in the development of spiritual health, by teachers in different school types.

Spiritual Facilitator

The notion of Spiritual Facilitator is my suggestion for action in schools in response to identified need in the area of nurturing spiritual health. As the development of relationships lies at the heart of spiritual health, the quality of people is of paramount importance in its promotion. Quality relates to all the valued characteristics of teachers detailed in preceding discussions. The teachers in my study stated their belief that the parents and families have primary responsibility for young people's spiritual health. They also agreed that the Principal either opens or closes the door to its inclusion in the ethos and practice of the school. The teachers expressed views that students can progressively take responsibility for the development of their own spiritual well-being. But, they need guidance and nurture to help develop the necessary foundation for this life-long journey. The quality of their teachers plays an enormous part in the development or destruction of this foundation for their lives.

All the teachers believed that spiritual health should be included in the school curriculum, in a variety of ways. The teachers, as the living curriculum, at times enhance, at other

Table 9. Valued teacher characteristics by school type

School type/ characteristic	Whole sample	State ($n = 18$)	Catholic ($n = 19$)	Other Christian ($n = 46$)	Other non-government ($n = 9$)
caring/sensitive/ personal	70%	72	74	74	**45**
concern for individual	68%	**78**	79	*54*	66
beliefs/values	57%	**17**	52	**70**	**78**
confident	41%	*39*	*39*	**26**	56
good teacher	37%	39	*53*	*32*	*33*
dedicated	37%	*33*	47	39	**11**
communication	22%	22	*16*	24	22
personable	20%	*0*	11	**32**	*11*
calm	16%	**28**	**26**	*13*	22

Note: Figures represent percentage of that *group* whose comments were attributed to the stated characteristic. Bold Figures represent > 10% variation from whole sample response, italics represent <whole sample value.

times hinder the students' spiritual health. More than two-thirds of the teachers expressed the view that spiritual health should be integral to all areas of the curriculum. The others wanted it in core and specific studies, because many were concerned that if everyone was responsible for fostering students' spiritual health; maybe no-one would end up really taking responsibility for it.

Just as Nolan postulated the 'need to re-introduce "spirituality" into the language of nursing' (Nolan & Crawford, 1997, p. 293), it is also 'difficult for [teachers as well as] nurses to acknowledge their own spirituality, which is essential if they are to nurture their clients [students]' (ibid.). Having a Spiritual Facilitator in each school could help ensure the staff were made aware, and were adequately prepared personally and professionally to effect programs most suited to foster their students' spiritual health, as part of their overall concern for students' well-being. The Spiritual Facilitator should not try to be the sole provider of opportunities for spiritual enhancement in a school. The role would be one of enabling, working with a wide range of people to have maximum impact on each area of progress in the students' lives. I believe that the Spiritual Facilitator could work with:

- the Principal, to review school policy statements and ensure that public pronouncements cohere with sound spiritual principles. The Spiritual Facilitator would need to be secure enough personally to be able to counsel the Principal (and staff) if their life examples and spoken words were causing conflict, or hindrance to the nurture of students' spiritual well-being.
- the Professional Development and Staff Welfare Coordinators to identify staff needs, enable counselling, plan and effect appropriate staff in-service activities, in-house and externally, for individuals, small and large groups. SuiTable reading material could also be made available for staff development.
- the Curriculum Coordinator and other Heads, to do regular curriculum audits to plan for the inclusion of activities, discussions, excursions, and camps to maximize opportunities for fostering students' spiritual health, as well as monitor progress.

- the Student Welfare, Pastoral Care, Religious Education Coordinators and Chaplain to develop procedures to enhance relationships in and out of class, in sports, assemblies, and clubs, to help the promotion of students' spiritual wellbeing.
- parents, in conjunction with other relevant staff, to facilitate communication between school and home, especially to help students identified as having relationship problems. Maybe some parenting programs could be offered as well, for example, Parent Effectiveness Training.
- community groups to provide opportunities for students to extend their interests in religious and/or environmental activities.

Spiritual Facilitators need to be secure in their own philosophy of life to foster discussions with other staff, students, parents and community leaders, to make each person feel valued, because of who they are, while allowing freedom of choice for movement to higher ideals on the pathway of life, taking every opportunity for enhancing their own and others' spiritual health.

If teachers are really concerned about the well-being of young people, should not students in all schools be given the opportunity to evaluate freely the traditions from which they come, and others of the community of which they are a part? Should not denominational schools be able to welcome representatives of other faiths to enrich multicultural dialogue, for edification of the future leaders of our society, namely our current students? If the beliefs of the schools are not strong enough to be questioned respectfully, they need to be. This includes the secular humanism which appears to be held almost sacrosanct in many State schools. The Spiritual Facilitator would have the responsibility of helping to maintain a balance, of encouraging teachers to be inspirational, getting students to question their philosophy of life, whilst identifying and curbing any excesses which did not allow freedom of choice by the students, from responsible alternatives.

As I envisage the role, the Spiritual Facilitator would have the task of overseeing the development of the knowledge and inspirational aspects of each of the four sets of relationships which comprise spiritual well-being in four domains of human existence, namely:

- the Personal-with a search for meaning, purpose, values, peace, and self-esteem;
- the Communal-embracing relationships, morality, culture, and religion;
- the Environmental-awareness and awe;
- the Global-looking beyond humanity to a Transcendent Other.

In so doing, conditions should exist to optimize the help and reduce the hindrances to the development of students' spiritual health in schools.

Acknowledgements

I appreciate the input by Associate Professor David Clarke and Dr. Murray Seiffert, who supervised my PhD, from which this paper is extracted. This article is based on a paper presented at the conference on '*Education, Spin'tuality and the Whole Child: Getting the message?*', Roehampton Institute, London, 20–21 June 1997.

References

Banks, R., Poehler, D. & Russell, R. (1984) Spirit and human-spiritual interaction as a factor in health and health education, *Health Education,* 15(5), pp. 16–19.

Bellingham, R., Cohen, B., Jones, T. & Spaniol, L. (1989) Connectedness: Some skills for spiritual health, *American Journal for Health Promotion,* 4(1), pp. 18–24, 31.

Benneti, D. & Nutbeam, D. (1993) An Australian agenda for adolescent health in the 1990s. *Journal of Paediatrics and Child Health,* 29 (Suppl. 1), pp. S1–S2.

Bensley, L. J. (1996) Values and morals: Bridging the gap between knowledge and behavior, *Journal of Health Education,* 27(6), pp. 332–337.

Bensley, R. J. (1991) Defining spiritual health: A review of the literature, *Journal of Health Education,* 22(5), pp. 287–290.

Chapman, L. (1986) Spiritual health: A component missing from health promotion, *American Journal of Health Promotion,* 1(1), pp. 38–41.

Diaz, D. P. (1993) Foundations for spirituality: Establishing the viability of spirituality within the health disciplines, *Journal of Health Education,* 24(6), pp. 324–326.

Ellison, C. (1983) Spiritual well-being: Conceptualization and measurement, *Journal of Psychology and Theology,* 11(4), pp. 330–340.

Fisher, J. W. (1997) *Some teachers' views on the place of spiritual health in the school curriculum.* A paper presented at the conference on Education, Spirituality and the Whole Child: Getting the message? Roehampton Institute, London, 20–21 June 1997.

Fisher, J. W. (1998) *Spiritual Health: Its nature, and place in the school curriculum.* Unpublished PhD Thesis, The University of Melbourne, Australia.

Fahlberg, L. L. & Fahlberg, L. A. (1991) Exploring spirituality and consciousness with an expanded science: Beyond the ego with empiricism, phenomenology, and contemplation, *American Journal of Health Promotion,* 5(4), pp. 273–281.

Goodloe, R. & Arreola, P. (1992) Spiritual health: Out of the closet, *Health Education,* 23(4), pp. 221–226.

Goudzwaard, B. (1997) Towards a future of care, in: I. Lambert & S. Mitchell (Eds) *The Crnmbling Walls of Certainty-Towards a Chnstian critique of postmodernity and education,* pp. 40–49 (Sydney, The Centre for the Study of Australian Christianity).

Hawks, S., Hull, M., Thalman, R. & Richins, P. (l995) Review of spiritual health: Definition, role, and intervention strategies in health promotion, *American Journal of Health Promotion,* 9(5), pp. 371–378.

Hood Morris, L. E. (1996) A spiritual well-being model: Use with older women who experience depression, *Issues in Mental Health Nursing,* 17, pp. 439–455.

Jose, N. (1987) The silent gift: A project for spiritual health, *Journal of School Health,* 57(2), pp. 72–73.

Mceetya National Goals Taskforce (1998) *Australia's Common and Agreed Goals for Schooling in the Twenty-first century-A* discussion paper (May).

Nolan, P. & Crawford, P. (1997) Towards a rhetoric of spirituality in mental health care, *Journal of Advanced Nursing,* 26, pp. 289–294.

Osman, J. & Russell., R. (1979) The spiritual aspects of health, *Journal of School Health,* 49, p. 359.

Resnick, M., Harris, L. & Blum, R. (1993) The impact of caring and connectedness on adolescent health and well-being, *Journal of Paediatrics and Child Health,* 29 (Suppl. I), pp. S3-S9.

Ross, L. A. (1996) Teaching spiritual care to nurses, *Nurse Education Today,* 16, pp. 38–43.

Seaward, B. L. (1991) Spiritual wellbeing: A health education model, *Health Education,* 22(3), pp. 166–169.

Vanryn, M. & Heaney, C. (1997) Developing effective helping relationships in health education practice. *Health Education & Behaviour,* 26(6), pp. 683–702.

Wallace, A. G. (1997) Educating tomorrow's doctors: the thing that matters is that we really care, *Academic Medicine,* 72(4), pp. 253–258.

Westgate, C. E. (1996) Spiritual wellness and depression, *Journal of Counseling & Development,* 75(1), pp. 26–35.

Attentiveness for children: proposing a neo-confucian curriculum for preschool education

Sandra Wu and Charlene Tan

ABSTRACT

In this article, we propose a neo-Confucian curriculum for preschool education based on the writings of the neo-Confucian thinker Zhu Xi. Against the contemporary backdrop of a narrow emphasis on the academic assessment of children, we argue for an alternative approach that revolves around *jing*: the inner mental attentiveness to be true to one's good nature. We propose an adaption of Bronfenbrenner's ecological systems theory and Confucian hierarchy of cardinal relationships that progressively cultivate the good nature of children across the spheres of the self, family and community, country and the world. We further outline an integrated programme with corresponding developmental domains, types of relationships and Confucian virtues. The desired outcome is the manifestation of each child's innate goodness through attentiveness to routines and the habituation of moral values. A neo-Confucian curriculum adds to the existing literature on preschool educational approaches that are experiential, values-centric, interpersonal and holistic.

Introduction

The early years are a critical period where children grow and develop most rapidly in their lives. Researchers have noted that standardised testing has permeated preschool education, perpetuating an output-oriented culture that diminishes the purpose and value of education (Tan 2019a, 2019b, 2020; Wu and Wenning 2016). To be sure, the assessment of children is not necessarily detrimental. But any evaluation in early childhood education should benefit every child, and inform the planning and implementation of curriculum for children's learning needs. Beyond standardised testing, there is a wide range of qualitative and quantitative methods to document and assess children's learning such as learning stories, photo observations and developmental checklists. It takes on a negative connotation when child assessment becomes a mere numbers games. In a testing culture, preschools are pressured to strive towards getting high scores for young children, resulting in the schoolification of preschool education. Against a backdrop where the tyranny of numbers seems to reign in the global educational arena to quantify academic achievement (Ball 2015), we propose an alternative approach that is derived from the wisdom tradition of neo-Confucianism.

Drawing upon the neo-Confucian thinker Zhu Xi's programme for children, we put forward an adaption of Bronfenbrenner's ecological systems theory and Confucian hierarchy of cardinal relationships. We shall explain how this curriculum is aimed at progressively cultivating the virtue of *jing* (attentiveness) in children by developing their good nature across the spheres of the self, family and community, country and the world. We shall give details of this integrated programme by sketching out the corresponding developmental domains, types of relationships and Confucian virtues. Our neo-Confucian preschool model aims to move away from a narrow focus on academic achievement to foster the spiritual ideal of *jing* (attentiveness) in children. It is helpful to clarify, at the outset, what we mean by spirituality. Spirituality is fundamentally a distinctive capacity to make sense of oneself within a wider framework of meaning and as part of some larger whole (Minney 1991; Tan and Wong 2012). Spiritual ideals, it follows, are concepts that direct our attention beyond the mundane and the material towards what is transcendent and eternal (Carr 1995). Examples of spiritual ideals are self-awareness, beauty and a sense of awe. *Jing* (attentiveness) qualifies as a spiritual ideal as it is concerned with the inner and reflective aspects of human experience that go beyond the superficial, as we shall explain later. Our neo-Confucian curriculum is drawn from the educational thought of the neo-Confucian thinker Zhu Xi (1130–1200) who is known as the founder of neo-Confucianism (Hwang 2013). This article is divided into two main segments: an exposition of Zhu Xi's neo-Confucian curriculum and its implications for contemporary preschool education.

Zhu Xi's curriculum

Xiao Xue *(elementary or lesser learning)*

Among the Confucian thinkers, Zhu Xi stands out for devoting his writings to education for children. His educational programme for children is encapsulated in his treatise titled *Xiao Xue* (Elementary or Lesser Learning). This book is 'a most influential text in the early spread of the Neo-Confucianism', offering advice on not only education for children and infants but also 'prenatal influences in the womb' (de Bary and Bloom 1999, 803). In his preface to the book, Zhu Xi clarifies that his recommended curriculum for children does not originate from him but is passed down from the sages and worthies in ancient times. Stressing that 'there is no difference between past and present and nothing should ever keep one from practising them', his aim is to outline what he believes is the best education for children (de Bary and Bloom 1999, 804).

Two preliminary comments are needed at this juncture concerning Zhu Xi's views on the age group and gender of the target audience. First, elementary learning is meant for children aged eight to 14, as mentioned in the Preface of the *Xiao Xue*. But it appears that Zhu Xi is also open to having children younger than eight years old being educated. The *Xiao Xue* records that children in antiquity received an elementary education 'at an early age' (1.1) and were 'taught as soon as they were able to talk and eat' (1.9, all translations of the *Xiao Xue* are taken from Gardner 1990, unless otherwise stated). The second clarification is that Zhu Xi, reflecting the gendered social norms in his day, has in mind male children for formal schooling. During his time, it was socially unacceptable for girls to attend school; they were taught at home by their mothers or, for the minority of female descendants of aristocrats, by private tutors. Despite Zhu Xi's presupposition of educating only boys, there is nothing in his philosophical and educational theories, worldviews and presuppositions that discriminates girls and prohibits schooling for them. As we shall see later, his ontological positions on innate human goodness, moral self-cultivation and potential for sageliness actually support education for both boys and girls since they apply to all human beings regardless of gender.

Jing as attentiveness

At the heart of Zhu Xi's elementary learning is the spiritual ideal of attentiveness (*jing*). We follow Graham (1958) and Gardner (1986) to gloss *jing* as attentiveness. Other translations of *jing* are mindfulness (de Bary 1981; Hwang 2013), seriousness (Chan 1989), inner mental composure (Gardner 1986) and reverence (Angle 2009) (for details, see Tan 2019c). According to Zhu Xi, *jing* essentially refers to the inner mental attentiveness to be true to one's good nature (1.8). In his words, *jing* is about 'mak[ing] the proper effort in all matters everywhere' (1.8). Commenting on the virtues of sage-kings such as Yao and Shun, Zhu Xi avers that they 'were attentive from beginning to end' and that they 'take inner mental attentiveness as the foremost of the virtues' (1.8). Integral to attentiveness is truthfulness (*cheng*): Zhu Xi writes that the curriculum enacted by the ancients 'fostered truthfulness and inner mental attentiveness in young children' (1.3). Truthfulness, also rendered sincerity, is about being true to one's nature by 'keeping one's original mind unified, free from deception' (Gardner 1990, 89). Truthfulness is preserved through a state of mind that is devoted to keeping one's original heart-mind unified without deception (Gardner 1990). That attentiveness is the pivot of elementary learning is seen in it being mentioned throughout *Xiao Xue*. For example, Zhu Xi maintains that the ancients 'simply attended to the mind, and this culminated in the good governance of the empire – everything flowed from the mind' (1.2). He expands on the ideal of attentiveness in 1.7: 'Only if they're [children] taught to regard inner mental attentiveness as central and to discipline their bodies and minds will they be capable of making the proper effort'. This passage informs us that attentiveness is not just about one's mental function but also physical involvement. Attentiveness, in a nutshell, synthesises one's cognitive, affective and behavioural engagement so that one can be true to one's inborn nature.

Attentiveness is premised on a neo-Confucian belief that human nature is good. Zhu Xi teaches that the objective of inculcating attentiveness in children is to manifest their 'germs of goodness' (1.3). The 'germs of goodness', as explained by Gardner (1990), is 'derived from Mencius' discussion of the "four germs" (2A/6) and refers to man's innately good nature' (89). The four germs or beginnings (*si duan*), according to Mencius, are *ren* (benevolence or an achieved state of humanity), *yi* (appropriateness), *li* (rituals or normative behaviours) and *zhi* (wisdom). These germs, believed by Mencius to be innate in all human beings, do not mean that humans are already morally perfect. Rather, as suggested by the word 'germs' (*duan*), these attributes are only in their incipient phase and can be beclouded by selfish desires. All human beings therefore have the responsibility to develop the germs of goodness and bring them to completion (Tan 2018). That is why education, particularly learning for children, is indispensable: nurture is needed to complement nature so that the germs of goodness in humans can grow and bear fruits.

Zhu Xi's curriculum for children

Zhu Xi delineates his curriculum for children in his Preface to *Xiao Xue*:

> In the elementary learning of ancient times, instruction followed the steps of "sprinkling and sweeping, listening and responding, advancing and retiring [in the presence of others'," as well as the loving of parents, respecting of elders, honouring of teachers, and being intimate with friends. All of these constituted the basis for cultivating the self, regulating the family, ordering the state, and bringing peace to all-under-Heaven. (translated by de Bary and Bloom 1999).

It can be observed from the above that an attentiveness-centred curriculum is experiential, values-centric and interpersonal. Rather than theoretical learning, the curriculum foregrounds physical activities such as sprinkling and sweeping. It is evident that the thrust of elementary learning is applied learning where children learn by doing (Tan 2019c). Zhu Xi underscores the importance of helping children to be 'personally familiar with many matters' (1.2) and gain 'the direct understanding of such-and-such an affair' (1.4). Zhu Xi explains the rationale of experiential learning in the Preface:

> Thus they were sure to be discussed and put into practice during the learner's younger years; in this way knowledge and discipline would grow together for the full development and transformation of the mind-and-heart, so that there would be no danger of conflict between nature and nurture (translated by de Bary and Bloom 1999).

The 'they' in the above passage refers to the contents of a *jing*-centred curriculum mentioned earlier, namely physical activities such as sprinkling and sweeping, and the inculcation of moral values such as loving their parents and being intimate with friends. Through human interactions ('listening and responding'), children learn, internalise and demonstrate moral values such as filial piety ('loving of parents'), respect ('honouring of teachers') and brotherhood ('being intimate with friends'). The mention of 'advancing and retiring in the presence of others' refers to 'the formalities of polite conversation and good manners' (Gardner 1990, 89) which affirms the importance of community living and enculturation for children. Demonstrating the Confucian accent on social embeddedness and human interdependence, Zhu Xi's curriculum situates the self as tied to one's family, state and the whole world.

A *jing*-centred curriculum, according to Zhu Xi, is also holistic. He lists in the preface of the *Xiao Xue* the 'six arts' (*liu yi*) that children need to learn. They are rituals, music, archery, charioteering, calligraphy, and mathematics. It should be pointed out that 'rituals' (*li*), for Zhu Xi and Confucians in general, are not limited to religious rites and social etiquette. Rather, rituals are understood broadly to encompass 'all the multifarious social norms that govern how we interact with one another' (Angle 2011, 186). A more accurate rendering of *li*, in our view, is normative behaviours that take place in our everyday life. Normative behaviours proceed from and reflect a person's moral values, attitudes and dispositions.

Zhu Xi's justification for an applied and values-driven curriculum is that learners, in their formative years, need to be habituated into certain thoughts, feelings and actions that will shape their character for life. Returning to Zhu Xi's theory of the innately good nature in all humans, the curriculum in elementary learning is targeted at enabling children to bring out and expand their germs of goodness. A *jing*-centred curriculum harmonises nature and nurture: such a curriculum directs the children to concentrate whole-heartedly on being true to their innate goodness (nature) through experiential learning in communal settings (nurture). It is instructive that Zhu Xi, in the above passage, refers to the full development and transformation of the mind-and-heart. The mind-and-heart (*xin*) in Confucian parlance refers to the seat of consciousness and moral conscience, unifying the cognitive and affective components of human awareness (Ching 1986; Tan 2013; Tu 1985). In sum, a *jing*-centred curriculum provides a disciplined, structured, values-based and social platform for children to transform their mind-and-heart so that they will be ready for *Da Xue* (Great Learning) at 15 years old and proceed to act spontaneously and ethically for the rest of their lives (Angle 2011).

It is apparent that a *jing*-centred curriculum as envisaged by Zhu Xi stands in opposition to the current fixation with academic achievement for children as exemplified in 'standardised testing'. It is noteworthy that Zhu Xi highlights and repudiates the injurious effects of high-stakes exam in his day. He asserts that 'preparing for the examinations has ruined so many people' (translated by

Angle 2009, 136); he also takes issue with 'memorisation and literary composition, which took double the exertion of the elementary education but was of no real use' (translated by de Bary and Bloom 1999, 724). What is unfortunately neglected in exam-oriented teaching and learning, according to Zhu Xi, is the child's self-development and moral cultivation (Tan 2019b, 2019c; de Bary and Chaffee 1989; Lior 2018). Having introduced Zhu Xi's curriculum for children that revolves around attentiveness, the next section gives an overview of curriculum models in preschool education.

Curriculum models in preschool education

Preschool education occurs in the first eight years of a child's life and is a period of learning and development that overlaps with elementary learning. In preschool education around the world, there are many different curriculum models such as Montessori model, project or inquiry-based approach, Reggio Emilia-inspired programmes, Multiple Intelligences model, High Scope curriculum, Steiner approach, play-based learning and emergent curriculum that are adopted in both Asian and Western societies (Wu 2017, 2018; Yang and Li 2019a). The theories, pedagogies and programmes that underpin these models originate from Western-European contexts which, through globalisation, are borrowed and adapted in different societies (Yang and Li 2019a; Wu and Wenning 2016). As such, the socio-cultural conception of preschool education is negotiated between the influence of western culture and the culture specific to the society that adopted these models, which consequently shape the beliefs surrounding children's identity as learners, their learning processes and own beliefs about their learning (Li). After all, humans are 'products of their own learning and the carriers of the entire human cultural heritage' (Li , 25). In the next segment, we propose an integrated programme for early childhood education that applies Zhu Xi's *jing*-centred curriculum to contemporary times.

Jing-centred curriculum as an integrated programme

Instead of being preoccupied with test scores and standardised assessments, Zhu Xi's *jing*-centred curriculum plays up the development of inner mental attentiveness and truthfulness to one's good nature. Such a curriculum offers an integrated programme for preschool education that features applied knowledge, values-inculcation, social interactions and all-rounded development. The desired outcome is to promote and support children's cultivation of their selves as whole persons through a developmentally appropriate programme. To put it simply, a *jing*-centred curriculum offers a structure for children to channel their inner attentiveness so as to draw out their germs of goodness. To achieve this goal, children need to learn and develop at different ages and stages in the first eight years of their lives according to the five domains of development –

physical, cognitive, social, emotional and linguistic. It is critical to keep in mind that all children develop sequentially in the milestones of each domain but may develop at different rates at each age and stage of their lives. As such, teachers need to be intentional when designing the schedule, activities and learning experiences as well as know each child intimately for effective lesson planning and implementation. The quality of this programme hinges on the quality of teachers as they are the direct implementers of the curriculum. These teachers need to possess a deep knowledge of the neo-Confucian philosophy, child development and early childhood pedagogies to facilitate holistic learning beyond the academics. The social and moral aspects of education are just as important.

To shed more light on the contemporary relevance of Zhu Xi's curriculum, it is instructive to compare it with Bronfenbrenner's ecological systems theory. Mapping Bronfenbrenner's (1994) and Bronfenbrenner and Morris (1998)) ecological systems theory to children's development, preschool education begins at the micro level, starting with children's development of their sense of self. This is reinforced by the relationships children have with their families and the community at the meso level. It is evident that the quality of relationships is crucial to children's learning and development. Over time, children's knowledge, skills and values will deepen and they will come to develop a sense of citizenship, loyalty and sense of duty towards their country at the exo level. This theory aligns with Zhu Xi's order of the essential relationships of 'ruler-subject, father-son, elder-younger brother, husband-wife, and friend-friend' (Zhao 2010, 587) (see Figure 1).

As noted earlier, Zhu Xi, evincing a Confucian viewpoint, emphasises the interests of the collective whole over individualistic self interests. Accordingly, self cultivation can only be achieved through interdependent relationships as the child progresses into adulthood. At preschool, children will learn about the preordained order of social hierarchy and how to place the interests of others above self in each of the five cardinal relationships. From a developmental perspective, young children tend to be egocentric in early childhood and would require time, education and positive reinforcement to mature and attain the goal of self actualisation and putting others before self. Progressively, there will be a shift from self centeredness to other centeredness that will allow them to transcend a pure focus on themselves as they engage in self-realisation.

Underpinning a neo-Confucian preschool educational model is an image of the child who is innately good, reflective and self-cultivating (Angle 2011; Zhao 2010; Bai 2005). The innate goodness in every child is premised on the child's cultivation of virtues such as 'benevolence, righteousness, courteousness and wisdom' for 'the formation and development of [one's] moral character' (Wang 2004, 430). The child cultivates virtues through one's interactions and relationships with others, beginning with one's relationship with one's parents. Filial piety undergirds the parent-child relationship which lays 'the foundation of all

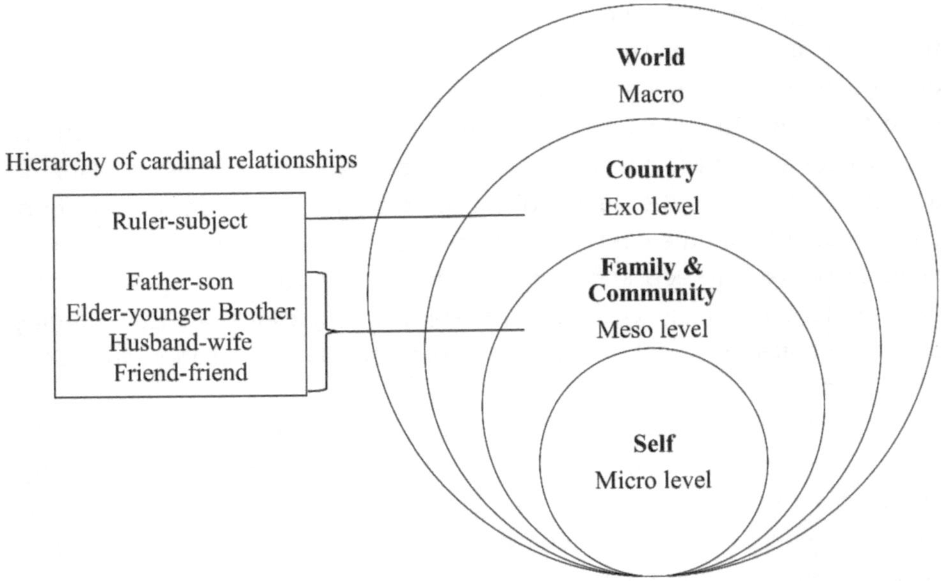

Figure 1. Adaptation of Bronfenbrenner's ecological systems theory and Confucian hierarchy of cardinal relationships.

virtues' and forms the basis of one's 'morality in order to fully realise benevolence' (Wang 2004, 432). It is an important part of a child's ethical education as it facilitates the child's development of other virtues. Coupled with a personal commitment to learning, the child strives towards a lifelong pursuit of achieving self-transformation (Cline 2015b; Yang and Li 2019b).

Figure 2 provides an overview of a *jing*-centred curriculum for preschool education that combines the fundamental tenets of the programme: curriculum, developmental domains, relationships and virtues. Anchored upon attentiveness, the programme facilitates the child's learning under the education and care of one's teachers in the first eight years of one's life within the context of interpersonal relationships. This model aligns with Zhu Xi's belief that education should be designed in such a way as to enable the child to practise attentiveness at all stages.

In this curriculum, children participate in activities that are developmentally appropriate for the different ages and stages of their lives to receive the care and education they need for optimal growth and development. The focal point of all activities is the nurture of a *jing* disposition through routinised and well-structured daily activities. The variety and intensity of activities depend on the curriculum and teacher. The intentional teacher will plan the curriculum according to children's interests and learning needs, and provide opportunities for them to explore and learn about their own country and culture, and the global society at large. The curriculum, in a nutshell, is both cultural and multicultural, local and global (Wu, Tan, and Ng 2020).

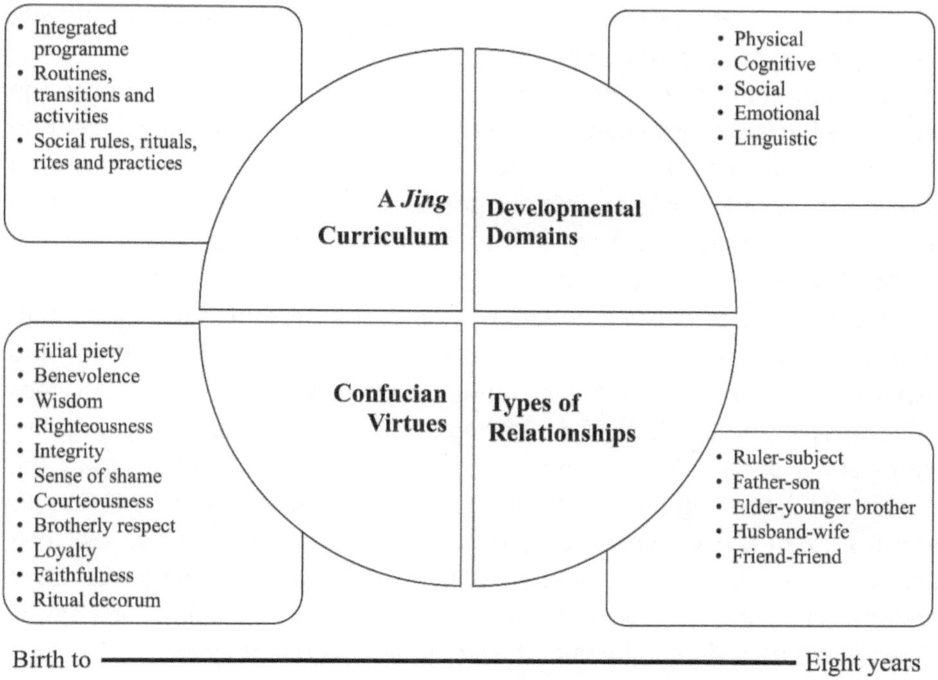

Figure 2. A *Jing* (Attentiveness) curriculum for preschool education.

Routines, transitions and activities

To further understand the *jing*-centred integrated programme for children, it is instructive to give details on the schedule that indicates the routines, transitions and activities for each age group. Having a fixed schedule provides the structure and predictability that young children need so that they will know what to expect throughout the day at their preschool.

The development of *jing* begins at infancy as a baby comes under the care and supervision of their educarers in a warm and cosy environment. The infant experiences love and learns about the world through the responsive, respectful and reciprocal relationships one has with the people in one's life. In the first year, the child would have already learnt about the different relationships such as familial and community ties, and friendships with one's parents, siblings, family members, caregivers, educarers, teachers and other children (Bronfenbrenner 1994; Cline 2015b). At this stage, the babies are dependent on their caregivers and/or educarers; an educarer is one who educates and takes care of the learning and developmental needs of the children under one's charge. Apart from being fed and napping, children would learn and practise different skills in each of the developmental domains which they will hone through repetition. The responsibility is shared between the preschool and home settings to facilitate the continuity of care because education takes place in the realm of relationships (Zhao

2010). As such, early relationships play a significant role in a child's growth, learning trajectory and outcomes.

The cultivation of *jing* continues as the child progresses into toddler age where the focus is on experiential learning. The toddler learns to direct attention to and gain control over one's body and movements, thereby developing simple and complex skills in different domains. For example, a child develops attentiveness through learning simple and complex fine motor skills, such as holding a spoon and subsequently using chopsticks; as well as gross motor skills when she is able to balance herself, walk and sit independently. She demonstrates language skills when she is able to communicate with others, and expresses her thoughts and feelings through words and actions. She develops thinking skills and builds on them through her everyday experiences. She also learns about social etiquette and personal hygiene such as putting away the crockery and cleaning her mouth and hands after a meal. Meal times usually transit into an activity, where children would need to listen and follow their teacher's instructions in an orderly manner. This involves cognition, which is understanding and processing the instructions; and self-regulation and control, which is the behavioural domain of learning as children obey instructions and abide by classroom rules.

The objective at this stage is to bring out the innate goodness and imbue moral values such as honouring one's teacher and disciplining oneself through experiential learning, as intended by Zhu Xi. This approach is aligned with theories of cognitive and moral development by Piaget (1932) and Kohlberg (1969, 1981), and social learning theory by Bandura and Walters (1963), which are dominant in early childhood education. But what makes the *jing*-centred curriculum outlined here different from the before-mentioned theories is the cultivation of attentiveness and its infusion into all aspects of the preschool curriculum. Given that children learn best through play, repetition and doing, there would be a variety of learning experiences designed for children at every age group. Zhu Xi calls for activities that will nurture children's innate goodness and indirectly eliminate their weakness. Songs and rhymes are a part of this curriculum which includes other activities that allow children to develop holistically. An attentiveness-centred, integrated programme supports the learning and development of different learning areas and domains in children's activities. For example, a simple activity such as jumping ropes in a group of three does not only focus on gross motor skills such as body and hand-eye coordination. These tasks also require children to practise prosocial skills such as communicating and collaborating with others, taking turns to jump and swing the rope. The performance of these competencies requires not just physical concentration but also corresponding mental and emotional attentiveness. They will also learn the value of developing friendships through teamwork, mutual respect and effective communication. From this, it is evident that one activity can cater to many different learning areas and the inculcation of virtues. The above activities will help children to regard inner mental attentiveness as central and to discipline their bodies and minds, as advocated by Zhu Xi.

Social rules, rituals and practices

Besides routines, transitions and activities, learning for children in the *jing*-centred curriculum also takes place in the context of human relationships. In each of the relationships children have formed, there is a set of social rules, rituals and practices to be learnt and followed. Rituals or normative behaviours are a form of moral education which teaches children good habits, conduct and norms that govern social interactions (Wang 2004; Angle 2011). They are also a form of discipline instructed and enforced by authorities such as parents, teachers and elders (Angle 2011). As such, teachers play an important role in educating children about the social rules, procedures and practices that they have to follow. Teachers also set boundaries so that children learn about what is permissible and not, and what is right and wrong. According to Zhu Xi, moral practice is a consistent, daily practice as 'moral behaviour can be satisfactory when a person is vigilant, reflective and approaches practice with caution' and it would not be satisfactory 'if a person practises moral behaviour leisurely' (Wang 2004, 431). Hence, self-discipline and good habits of conduct are cultivated from early childhood so that bad conduct could be eliminated (Wang 2004).

Through positive education, the child will learn to uphold one's duty as an individual first, then as a citizen, son/daughter, brother/sister, husband/wife and friend in accordance to the order of relationships and prescribed social rules. In the process, the child's mind-and-heart will be transformed incrementally (Wang 2004; Angle 2011). At preschool, teachers explicitly teach and model desirable behaviours and the acceptable code of conduct (Angle 2011). Children learn and practise respect and courteousness through rituals such as greeting their teachers and peers in class, inviting everyone to eat together during meal times, using words such as 'please' and 'thank you'. Such acts of respect are in line with the virtue of courteousness that children should acquire in school. These rituals are reinforced by the social hierarchy at home, in school and the society at large, which follows the order and power dynamics of cardinal relationships.

At home, it could be the daily exchanges of greetings such as parents teaching their child from infancy her name by addressing her with her given name and identifying themselves as her father and mother. As the child grows, she would learn of the names or terms that she should use to address her family members by, for example, paternal and maternal grandparents, uncles and aunties, brothers and sisters according to the family hierarchy (Cline 2015a). Recall that Zhu Xi recommends teaching young children about doing household chores such as sweeping and the rituals of loving their families, respecting their parents and teachers, being courteous and on good terms with their friends (Wang 2004). Practising such tasks and social etiquette will prepare children for the six arts that support their moral practice (Angle 2011; Bai 2005). The practices which are cultivated at home should be reinforced in school so that children continue to experience 'the direct understanding of a given affair' as envisaged by Zhu Xi (Angle 2011, 185).

Role of the educator

The successful enactment of the *jing*-centred curriculum for children is impossible without the critical role of the educators. In the preschool setting, teachers inculcate virtues in young children through storytelling by using questioning skills to develop children's thinking and moral values. Stories are not merely for literary pleasure; they also help children to understand life through literature and are an important aspect of children's ethical development and formation of worldview (Angle 2011). Over time, children learn about cultures and values, moral dilemmas, good and bad characters and develop moral reasoning which they will use to decide how they should conduct themselves. They will be equipped to go about their lives according to the values and virtues taught to them and aspire to achieve sagehood, as manifested through their mastery of normative behaviours that signify excellence in character (Angle 2011; Cline 2015a). For example, the children's story on 'The Boy Who Cried Wolf' is an Aesop fable that teaches children the dire consequences of false alarm. This story is appropriate to inculcate the virtues of truthfulness and inner mental attentiveness in young children so that they can keep their original mind unified and free from deception.

While preschool education is mostly planned and implemented by teachers, there are also teachable moments and learning opportunities in daily experiences that serve to foster attentiveness in children. After all, moral cultivation does not only occur in the classroom or through formal lessons, but is also integrated into the activities and interactions of children's everyday life (Cline 2015b). As early as early childhood, it is inevitable for children to avoid challenge and difficulties such as disagreeing with peers or encountering a problem during play. These unplanned moments serve as opportunities for children to apply what they have learnt through trial and error and resolve the issues faced. For instance, when children play in a group, they would need to exercise communication and social skills. When they encounter a conflict with others, they would need to pull together their problem-solving and negotiation skills and exercise empathy to see things from the perspective of others so as to reach an amicable mutual agreement for conflict resolution.

In sum, the desired outcome of a *jing*-centred curriculum is in line with Bandura and Walters' (1963) social learning theory where the acquisition of moral standards is a 'gradual process of imitating the observable values and behaviours of others' (Cowan et al. 1969, 261). Zhu Xi's curriculum is also in tandem with Piaget's (1932) cognitive theory of moral development which espouses that children develop moral judgements and construct their own ethical positions progressively by resolving moral dilemmas through a sequence of stages that contributes to their moral development (Cowan et al. 1969). According to Piaget (1932), social interactions are an important factor in children's development of moral understanding and autonomy. Children participate in different types of relationships that emphasise respect for and authority of parents; and mutual reciprocity and cooperation with peers that result in the learning of moral rules and the emergence of subjective morality (Cowan et al. 1969; Carpendale 2000). The *jing*-centred curriculum described here is also supported by Colby and Kohlberg's (1987) theory of moral reasoning. Colby and Kohlberg (1987) posit that children progressively develop moral reasoning through perspective taking, accumulated through life experiences of conflict resolution and managing moral dilemmas, which over time, enable them to cultivate autonomy and recognise the importance of treating one another as free and equal autonomous persons towards the ideal of making moral decisions for the common good of all involved (Carpendale 2000).

Overall, a model of preschool education that adheres to Zhu Xi's *jing*-centred curriculum harmonises a child's cognitive, affective and behavioural engagement so that one can be true to one's inborn nature. At each stage of their growth, children should 'discipline their bodies and minds' (1.7) by being watchful over of their thoughts, feelings and actions in daily life.

Conclusion

Early childhood begins from birth and sets the important foundation for children's later trajectory in elementary learning when they reach the age of eight. One of the objections for starting standardised testing too early in a child's life is the schoolification of preschool education – where the focus is on academic learning before children are developmentally ready (Shuey et al. 2019). Since 2017, the far reaching effects of Organisation for Economic Co-operation and Development's (OECD) standardised testing have been felt at the early years with the launch of the International Early Learning and Childhood Well-being Study (IELS), also colloquially referred to as the 'baby PISA'. PISA stands for Programme for International Student Assessment – an influential global yardstick to measure the quality of education systems around the world by testing the skills and knowledge of 15-year -old students in reading, mathematics and science (OECD 2018). Baby PISA assesses five-year-old children's emergent literacy, emergent numeracy, social and emotional skills using standardised measures (OECD 2017). There are 140 countries committed to the UN convention on the rights of the child (United Nations 2019) and 79 countries that have participated in PISA that occurs every three years (Organisation for Economic Co-operation and Development (OECD) 2018).

Against the contemporary backdrop of a narrow emphasis on the academic assessment of children, we argue for an alternative approach that centres on attentiveness. It is pertinent that there has been a revival of Confucian education in Chinese societies in recent years (Wu and Wenning 2016). It follows that other than the dominant Western-European ideas that are prevalent in the education landscape, Chinese philosophies can and should also be adapted. Focusing on a neo-Confucian curriculum, this paper has expounded on the spiritual ideal of attentiveness for children. . Zhu Xi's curriculum revolves around the virtue of *jing* that refers to the inner mental attentiveness to be true to one's good nature. The desired outcome is the manifestation of each child's innate goodness through routines and the habituation of moral values. We explained that a *jing*-centred curriculum is enacted through an integrated programme that is experiential, values-centric, interpersonal and holistic. A *jing*-centred curriculum enables children to develop their physical, cognitive, social, emotional and linguistic domains.

Zhu Xi's curriculum, including the spiritual ideal of spirituality and Confucian virtues in general, are secular and universal in nature. Rather than creating a dichotomy between Western and Asian values, these values can be cultivated in children through the different types of relationships that children have in the culture and society that they live in. Furthermore, it is precisely because their learning takes place in social settings where they internalise and exhibit cardinal Confucian virtues such as benevolence and righteousness that such an education must start at early childhood and continue into higher levels of education in order for a child to fully realise oneself.

Disclosure statement

No potential conflict of interest was reported by the authors.

References

Angle, S. C. 2009. *Sagehood: The Contemporary Significance of neo-Confucian Philosophy*. Oxford: Oxford University Press.

Angle, S. C. 2011. "A Productive Dialogue: Contemporary Moral Education and Zhu Xi's neo-Confucian Ethics." *Journal of Chinese Philosophy* 38: 183–203. doi:10.1111/j.1540-6253.2012.01696.x.

Bai, L.-M. 2005. "Children at Play: A Childhood beyond the Confucian Shadow." *Childhood*, 12 (1), 9–32. SAGE Publications. doi:10.1177/0907568205049890.

Ball, S. J. 2015. "Education, Governance and the Tyranny of Numbers." *Journal of Education Policy* 30 (3): 299–301. doi:10.1080/02680939.2015.1013271.

Bandura, A., and Walters, R. H. 1963. "Social learning and personality development." Holt Rinehart and Winston: New York

Bronfenbrenner, U. 1994. "Ecological Models of Human Development." In *International Encyclopaedia of Education*. edited by, M. Gauvain and M. Cole, 37–43. New York: Freeman. Retrieved from http://www.columbia.edu/cu/psychology/courses/3615/Readings/BronfenbrennerModelofDevelopment(short%20version).pdf

Bronfenbrenner, U., and P. A. Morris. 1998. "The Ecology of Developmental Processes." In *Handbook of Child Psychology: Vol 1. Theoretical Issues*, edited by W. Damon, 993–1028. New York: Wiley.

Carpendale, J. I. M. 2000. "Kohlberg and Piaget on Stages and Moral Reasoning." *Developmental Review* 20 (2): 181–205. doi:10.1006/drev.1999.0500.

Carr, D. 1995. "Towards a Distinctive Conception of Spiritual Education." *Oxford Review of Education* 21 (1): 83–98. doi:10.1080/0305498950210106.

Chan, W.-T. 1989. *Chu Hsi: New Studies*. Honolulu, HI: University of Hawaii Press.

Ching, J. 1986. "Chu Hsi on Personal Cultivation." In *Chu Hsi and Neo-Confucianism*, edited by W.-T. Chan, 273–291. Honolulu: University of Hawaii Press.

Cline, E. M. 2015a. "Moral Cultivation, Filial Piety, and the Good Society in Classical Confucian Philosophy." In *Families of Virtue: Confucian and Western Views on Childhood Development*. edited by, E. M. Cline, 1–27. University of Minnesota. Columbia Scholarship Online. 10.7312/Columbia/9780231171557.003.001.

Cline, E. M. 2015b. "Infants, Children, and Early Confucian Moral Cultivation." In *Families of Virtue: Confucian and Western Views on Childhood Development*. edited by, E. M. Cline, 1–35. University of Minnesota. Columbia Scholarship Online. 10.7312/Columbia/9780231171557.003.002.

Colby, A. and Kohlberg, L. 1987. "The measurement of moral judgment, Vol. 1." Theoretical foundations and research validation; Vol. 2. Standard issue scoring manual. Cambridge University Press

Cowan, P. A., J. Langer, J. Heavenrich, and M. Nathanson. 1969. "Social Learning and Piaget's Cognitive Theory of Moral Development." *Journal of Personality and Social Psychology* 11 (3): 261–274. doi:10.1037/h0027000.

de Bary, T. W., and J. W. Chaffee. 1989. *Neo-Confucian Education: The Formative Stage*. Berkeley: University of California Press.

de Bary, W. T. 1981. *Neo-Confucian Orthodoxy and the Learning of the Mind-and-Heart*. New York, NY: Columbia University Press.

de Bary, W. T., and I. Bloom. 1999. *Sources of Chinese Tradition: From Earliest Times to 1600*. 2nd ed. New York: Columbia University Press.

Gardner, D. K. 1986. *Chu Hsi and the Ta-hsueh: Neo-Confucian Reflection on the Confucian Canon*. Cambridge, MA,: Harvard University Press.

Gardner, D. K. 1990. *Learning to Be a Sage. Selections from the Conversations of Master Chu, Arranged Topically*. Berkeley, CA: University of California Press.

Graham, A. C. 1958. *Two Chinese Philosophers: Ch'eng Ming-Tao and Ch'eng Yi-ch'uan*. London,: Lund Humphries.

Hwang, K. 2013. "Educational Modes of Thinking in Neo-Confucianism: A Traditional Lens for Rethinking Modern Education." *Asia Pacific Education Review* 14 (2): 243–253. doi:10.1007/s12564-013-9243-3.

Kohlberg, L. 1969. "Stage and sequence: The cognitive-developmental approach to socialization." In D. Goslin (Ed.), Handbook of socialization theory and research (pp. 347–480). New York: Rand McNally

Kohlberg, L. 1981. "The philosophy of moral development." New York: Harper & Row

Lior, Y. 2018. "Neo-Confucianism as a Guide for Contemporary Confucian Education." In *Confucianism Reconsidered: Insights for American and Chinese Education in the Twenty-first Century*, edited by X. Liu and W. Ma, 87–109. Albany: State University of New York Press.

Minney, R. 1991. "What Is Spirituality in an Educational Context?" *British Journal of Educational,* 39 (4): 386-397.

Organisation for Economic Co-operation and Development (OECD). (2017). "The International Early Learning and Child Well-being Study.." Retrieved from http://www.oecd.org/education/school/international-early-learning-and-child-well-being-study.htm

Organisation for Economic Co-operation and Development (OECD). 2018. "Pisa 2018." http://www.oecd.org/pisa

Piaget, J. 1932. "The moral judgment of the child."London: Kegan, Paul, Trench, Trubner & Co

Shuey, E., A. Kim, N. Cortazar, A. Poblete, X. Rivera, L. Lagos, M. J. Faverio, and F. A. Abd Engel. 2019. "Curriculum Alignment and Progression between Early Childhood Education and Care and Primary School: A Brief Review and Case Studies." *OECD Education Working Paper No. 193*. http://www.oecd.org/officialdocuments/publicdisplaydocumentpdf/?cote=EDU/WKP(2019)1&docLanguage=En

Tan, C. 2013. *Confucius*. London: Bloomsbury.

Tan, C. 2018. "Mencius' Extension of Moral Feelings: Implications for Cosmopolitan Education." *Ethics and Education* 14 (1): 70–83. doi:10.1080/17449642.2018.1538690.

Tan, C. 2019a. *Comparing High-Performing Education Systems: Understanding Singapore, Shanghai, and Hong Kong*. Oxon: Routledge.

Tan, C. 2019b. "Beyond the Competencies Agenda in Large-scale International Assessment: A Confucian Alternative." *Philosophical Inquiry in Education* 26 (1): 20–32.

Tan, C. 2019c. "Rethinking the Concept of Mindfulness: A neo-Confucian Approach." *Journal of Philosophy of Education* 53 (2): 359–373. doi:10.1111/1467-9752.12343.

Tan, C. 2020. "Beyond High-stakes Exam: A neo-Confucian Educational Programme and Its Contemporary Implications." *Educational Philosophy and Theory* 52 (2): 137–148. doi:10.1080/00131857.2019.1605901.

Tan, C., and Y.-L. Wong. 2012. "Promoting Spiritual Ideals through Design Thinking in Public Schools." *International Journal of Children's Spirituality* 17 (1): 25–37. doi:10.1080/1364436X.2011.651714.

Tu, W.-M. 1985. *Confucian Thought: Selfhood as Creative Transformation*. Albany, NY: State University of New York Press.

United Nations (UN). 2019. "UN Treaty Collection: Chapter IV Human Rights 11 Convention on the Rights of the Child." https://treaties.un.org/pages/ViewDetails.aspx?src=IND&mtdsg_no=IV-11&chapter=4&lang=en

Wang, F.-Y. 2004. "Confucian Thinking in Traditional Moral Education: Key Ideas and Fundamental Features." *Journal of Moral Education*, 33(4), 429–447. Carfax Publishing Company. doi:10.1080/0305724042000327984.

Wu, J.-T., and M. Wenning. 2016. "The Postsecular Turn in Education: Lessons from the Mindfulness Movement and the Revival of Confucian Academies." *Philosophy & Education* 35 (6): 551–571. doi:10.1007/s11217-016-9513-8.

Wu, P.-H. S. 2017. "*Exploring Pedagogical Leadership in the Early Childhood Context of Singapore*." PhD dissertation. Nanyang Technological University.

Wu, P.-H. S. 2018. "Translation of Language Policy from Pre-school to Primary School." In *Un(intended) Language Planning in a Globalising World: Multiple Levels of Players at Work*, edited by C. Chua, S. K. Chew, P. G. L. K. Taylor-Leech, and C. Williams, 267–289. Berlin: De Gruyter Open.

Wu, S., P.-H. C. Tan, and C. S. L. Ng. 2020. "Educating Multicultural Citizens from a Confucian Heritage: Examples from Singapore." In *Handbook of Research on Citizenship and Heritage Education*, edited by E. J. Delgado-Algarra and J. M. Cuenca-López, 500–524. Hershey, Pennsylvania: IGI Global.

Yang, W.-P., and H. Li. 2019a. "Early Childhood Curriculum Reforms in Chinese Societies." In *Early Childhood Curriculum in Chinese Societies - Policies, Practices, and Prospects*, edited by W.-P. Yang and H. Li, 23–37, Taylor & Francis Group.

Yang, W.-P., and H. Li. 2019b. "Comparing Early Childhood Curriculum Policies in Chinese Societies." In *Early Childhood Curriculum in Chinese Societies - Policies, Practices, and Prospects*, edited by W.-P. Yang and H. Li, 38–50, Taylor & Francis Group.

Zhao, G.-P. 2010. "Chinese Cultural Dynamics and Childhood: Towards a New Individuality for Education." *Frontiers of Education in China*, 5(4), 579–595. Springer Science & Business Media B.V. doi:10.1007/s11516-010-0117-8.

A conceptual investigation into the possibility of spiritual education

Ping Ho Wong

ABSTRACT
Three commonly mentioned aspects of the idea of spirituality are transcendence, raised awareness and spiritualism. The interrelationships among these three 'strands' of spirituality are explored. It is argued that each strand expresses itself along a continuum, ranging from the mundane to theprofound. The second part of the article focuses on the education of spirituality in the senses of tran- scendence and raised awareness. Language learning provides a model for making sense of the process of how spirituality might 'emerge' through some dedicated practice, just as meaning is eventually grasped with the initially meaningless deployment of the verbal form. The importance of a spiritual ethos for spiritual education is highlighted.

Into the maze of the concept of spirituality

To look into the possibility of spiritual education begs the question of what 'spiritual education' and, ultimately, 'spirituality' are understood to be. Despite the caution that 'attempted definition [of the spiritual] is not only futile but totally counter productive' because 'it is a characteristic of spirit and the spiritual that it is dynamic' (Priestley, 1985, p. 114), it is necessary to provide some brief indications of certain aspects of the idea of 'spirituality' with which I can personally connect, and which are also commonly included in various formulations of spirituality.

Transcendence

One commonly mentioned aspect of spirituality is transcendence. For example, Emmons puts 'the capacity to transcend the physical and the material' (1999, p. 164) at the head of his list of five characteristics displayed by spiritually intelligent individuals. While Emmons construes transcendence as being related 'to a person's capacity to engage in heightened or extraordinary forms of consciousness', such as 'rising above our natural world to relate with a divine being', or 'going beyond our physical state to effect a heightened awareness of ourselves' (1999, p. 164), I would venture to suggest that a more mundane form of transcendence is also possible, and indeed more common, which simply involves one's awareness of and commitment to values beyond the physical and material realms, or the pursuit of goals that go beyond the self.[1] The commitment to non-materialistic values and the pursuit of self-transcend- ing goals, in turn, give a sense of meaning and purpose to an individual's life, and are the sources (or at least, the close allies) of other features that are commonly associated with the concept of spirituality such as perseverance in the face of hardship and the capacity to be virtuous.

Raised awareness

Experiences that are profound or mystical, and heightened states of consciousness, are one area that has attracted the attention of a lot of researchers, William James being one of the most prominent among them. Hay with Nye (1998) put forward three 'categories of spiritual sensitivity': awareness sensing, which is 'characterized by a sharply focused attention to the here-and-now of one's experience' (Hay, 1995, p. 19); mystery sensing, which involves the 'awareness of aspects of our life experience that are in principle incomprehensible' (Hay with Nye 1998, p. 66); and value sensing, which is the direct perception of value and meaning. Furthermore, Nye's research with children highlighted the salience of 'relational consciousness'— the sense of oneness with the self, with people, with the world and with God—in children's spirituality (and probably not only in children's spirituality). Just as it is conceivable that there might be a 'spectrum of transcendence' ranging from the mundane to the extraordinary, so I would speculate that there are different degrees of 'mystical' experience too. Our ordinary experience is already mystical in a very dilute sense, and it is this weak but pervasive mystical quality of everyday experi- ence that provides the basis that makes it possible for us to make sense of descrip- tions of the heightened forms of these experiences that warrant the term 'mystical'. For example, an everyday conversation that opens up a space of intersubjectivity where two or more individuals engage each other in an encounter with open hearts and minds is a spiritual experience, in the sense that each participant has in some,albeit small, degree transcended himself or herself and achieved oneness with the other. Every act of understanding is a minor miracle. Admittedly, such a conversa- tion (and the understanding it makes possible) may fall far short of a genuine dialogue involving a full I–Thou relationship, a form of dialogue that is 'an unusual phenomenon, since the I meets the Thou merely by grace' (Yaron, 1993, p. 2).

However, this merely reinforces the point I wish to make: spirituality comes in different degrees and shades, like the colours in a colour circle, and for some purposes at least, no radical break should be assumed to exist between spiritual and unspiritual states such as the I–Thou and the I–It relationship. It is possible to imagine, Buber notwithstanding, a conversation that does not feature a full-fledged I–Thou relationship between the participants, and yet is not a totally I–It non-encounter.

Associations between spirituality as transcendence and spirituality as heightened states of consciousness are apparent. 'Raised awareness' (Hay with Nye, 1998) is transcendence of ordinary experience. The direct perception of value in a heightened state of consciousness transcends any intellectual appraisal of the pros and cons,committing one to the value thus perceived with the force of emotion and despite oneself (in a restricted sense of the self: see n.1, above). Similarly, an intuitive grasp of some profound meaning and point in existence provides the inexhaustible impetus for the dedicated pursuit of one's vocation. And the self is infinitely expanded or transcended in relational consciousness.

Spiritualism

Another domain that is also often denoted by the term 'spirituality' covers spiritual phenomena such as activities of the soul or spirit as distinct from the body in a separate spiritual realm, and contacts and interactions with spiritual entities or forces. It posits the literal reality of a spiritual plane of existence, as distinct from a metaphorical spiritual dimension of human existence. Again, I would like to suggest a continuum of 'spiritual phenomena' in this sense, from weak

> to strong. An example of a 'weak' spiritual stand would be the position labelled 'transpersonal, a term that Jung had coined to describe experiences in which we transcend our individual identities and tap into a "collective unconscious" shared by all humans'[2] (Horgan, 2003, p. 160). 'Stronger' spiritual positions might more properly be labelled spiritualist, paranormal or even occult, such as Rudolf Steiner's anthroposophy. This sense of 'spirituality' is related to the other two senses, in that both 'raised awareness' and the value and meaning deriving from and driving transcendence cry out to be further accounted for and made sense of,[3] and one plausible way in which this can be done is to posit a separate spiritual realm as the venue of mystical experiences, and where all ultimate values reside and emanate.

Perhaps all sincere spiritual pursuits would ultimately have to face up to and answer the question of the ontological underpinnings of mystical experiences and of meaning and value. However, in practice, the three 'strands' of spirituality can be addressed relatively separately. Very often, in investigations of mystical experiences and of meaning and value, the question of their ontological underpinnings is 'bracketed'. And the distinction between spirituality as mystical experience and spirituality as interactions with spiritual forces is blurred. For example, in *The secret spiritual world of children*, Hart (2003) has gathered together a wealth of accounts of children's spiritual experiences, one of which is about the interactions his daughter, Haley, had with her angel, who provided Haley with guidance. Hart himself raised the question of the ontological nature of such encounters: 'Does she really see an angel?' (2003, p. 22); 'Would it be more accurate to think of Haley's angel as part of herself, "a fountainhead from within"?' (p. 23). However, in the end, Hart evades (or, should we say, transcends?) the question he raises:

> The source of guidance and knowledge, like Haley's, may indeed be thought of as on the inside—an inner fountainhead—or on the outside—the muses of the ancient Greeks or maybe a guardian angel. What is most significant is not the concept we use to describe this knowing, but the fact that, by whatever name, it is available. Its value is measured by the quality of what is heard and how it impacts a life. Haley is able to tap a source of insight, loving comfort, and guidance. (Hart, 2003, p. 23)

In the adoption of an agnostic stance and the bracketing of the question of the reality of spiritual beings or spiritual forces, my own stand is similar to Hart's. And I will not even touch upon any paranormal experiences such as the one reported by Haley about her angel. This is controversial territory, and anyway I am temperamentally not attracted to such matters—but neither am I for the view that spiritual beings or forces definitely do not exist. There is simply insufficient ground for me to take any side. The most that I am comfortable to positively believe is that there is a voice in our heart telling us the right things to do—if only we can still ourselves, listen for its faint utterances and hear it.

The value of the mundane

To conclude, to me spirituality is the capability of and the disposition to transcendence and raised awareness, including relational consciousness (and human qualities and their manifestations associated with transcendence and raised awareness), with these terms being understood both in their mundane and profound senses. In practice, my emphasis would be on their mundane senses, since what I am concerned with is education, for most people, not just for a few spiritual geniuses. In focusing on the weak and mundane forms of spirituality, I may be accused of underestimating everyday folk's spiritual potentiality, and also of adopting a compromising and compromised position with regard to the properly stringent requirements of spirituality, a position that condones and encourages mediocrity, and is thus not spiritual at all. In my defence, I can only say that I do sincerely believe if we focus mostly on the profound expressions of spirituality, particularly as the aim of spiritual education, we run the risk of sacrificing the majority without necessarily benefiting the spiritual development of the few who do have the potential for great spiritual achievements.

Furthermore, even if I do indeed underestimate the everyday person's spiritual potentiality, my misguided estimation is made not out of arrogance and snobbery, but based on self-reflection. I do not think I can aspire to a profound spirituality featuring, for example, an exalted ultimate concern or intense mystical experiences. With regard to spiritual potentiality, I consider myself representative of, if not actually less 'spiritually intelligent' and more mediocre than, most people. And I do believe the mundane and 'weak' forms of spirituality are no less valuable than the profound forms, though probably they are valuable in slightly different ways.

What is 'spiritual education'?

As a corollary to my understanding of spirituality, spiritual education, in its broadest sense, would be any intended or unintended circumstance or effort that promotes the development and flourishing of spirituality, in particular, the capability of and the disposition to transcendence and raised awareness, including relational consciousness. Examples of qualities associated with these two forms of spirituality that should be promoted include commitment to non-materialistic values; pursuit of self-tran scending goals; a sense of meaning and purpose in life; perseverance and resilience in the face of hardship; being virtuous; the capacity to feel curiosity, wonder and awe, even in everyday life; and openness to relations.

The importance of social ethos 13

What forms can and should spiritual education take? The African proverb 'It takes a village to raise a child', popularized by Hillary Clinton's book, *It takes a village* (Clinton, 1996), provides a convenient entry point into our consideration of the issue.The proverb can, of course, be variously interpreted. It reminds us that 'raising the next generation is a shared responsibility' (Bateson, 2000, p. 153), requiring the active involvement of numerous people in the community. It also hints at the crucial role played by the social ethos in a child's education, a point well recognized in the Chinese tradition. The popular Chinese practice of consulting geomancy (*fengshui*) masters for the selection and arrangement of residence with a view to the promotion of prosperity and good fortune is now well known, but ever since antiquity the Chinese sages have been advising people about the careful choice of the community of residence based on a consideration not of its material, but its moral and spiritual impact on the residents. Confucius once remarked that 'It is Goodness[4] that gives to a neighbourhood its beauty. One who is free to choose, yet does not prefer to dwell among the Good—how can he be accorded the name of wise?' (Confucius, 2000, p.94) It is said that Mother Meng (Mencius's mother, who was widowed) moved the family three times in Mencius's childhood until they:

> lived next to a school. [The young] Mencius then played by setting up sacrificial utensils, and performing the rituals of a guest bowing, giving way, entering, and departing.Meng's mother said, 'Truly I can reside with my son here.' And so they lived there. (Wang, 2003, p.150)

Mencius's subsequent great achievements are said to have owed a great deal to his mother's wise choice of neighbourhood.

The proverb 'It takes a village to raise a child' can also be 'over-interpreted' as asserting the superiority and wholesomeness of the intimate ethos characteristic of a village community as an environment for children to grow up in. Tönnies, a nineteenth-century German sociologist, called such a village ethos *Gemeinschaft* ('community'), 'a state characterized by a sense of fellow feeling, strong personal ties, and sturdy primary memberships, along with a sense of personal loyalty to one another', in contradistinction to *Gesellschaft* ('society'), a condition that occurs when rural life is displaced by urban living, and is characterized by 'a high division of labour, less prominence of personal ties, the lack of a sense of community among the members of society, and the absence of a feeling of belonging' (Anderson & Taylor, 2000, p. 597). That this by-now globalized movement from rural to urban life, from *Gemeinschaft* to *Gesellschaft*, has greatly compromised the ability of the community to serve as a kind of pervasive 'hidden curriculum' for people's spiritual education, and, to put it even in stronger terms, has turned the community into an agent of spiritual mis-education that actively corrodes people's spirit, has frequently been observed, commented upon and lamented by people of different persuasions from a variety of perspectives, though not always using the term 'spirituality'. For example,

> Buber believed that there had been a movement from relation to separation, that there was a growing crisis of being or existence in 'modern' society. He believed that the relationship between individuals and their selves ... between people, and people and creation was increasingly that of I–It. As a result it was becoming more and more difficult to encounter God. (Smith, 2000, n.p.)

Of course the movement from rural to urban life is only one of many intertwined factors, such as the rapid development of technology and worldwide ideological developments that have culminated at the present point in time in the hegemony of neo-liberalism; and that have acted together to continually reshape the ethos and texture of contemporary social life in a modernized community, like Hong Kong, in such a way as to prompt some commentators to deploy the metaphors of poison and pollution to describe the current social and cultural environment. For example, the Vietnamese Buddhist monk Thich Nhat Hanh pointed out that:

> There is pollution in our consciousness. Television, films, and newspapers are forms of pollution for us and our children. They sow seeds of violence and anxiety in us and pollute our consciousness, just as we destroy our environment by farming with chemicals, clear cutting the trees, and polluting the water. We need to protect the ecology of the Earth and the ecology of the mind, or this kind of violence and recklessness will spill over into even more areas of life. (Thich, 1997, p. 165)

Garbarino (1995) offers a more systematic critique of the unwholesome social ethos, using the term 'socially toxic environment ... to suggest that the social context of children, the social world in which they live, has become poisonous to their development' (Garbarino,

1995, p. 3). The targets of his critique include television, the erosion of childhood as a protected social space, the decline of civility and the 'monetarization' of daily life, among others.

Limitations of a compartmentalized spiritual education

It is my belief that effective spiritual education is, first and foremost, rendered by the social ethos. By saying this, I do not mean there is no room for more or less 'compartmentalized' spiritual education initiatives, to be carried out in specific and more confined contexts, such as that of the school, including the school curriculum, in the form of a more narrowly defined spiritual education. After all, the social ethos is constituted by the sum of all individual actions, social relations and collective

undertakings—without forgetting the significant implications of the crucial fact that this whole thus constituted is larger than the sum of its parts. There is indeed an important role to be played by spiritual education initiatives and activities, for example, sessions set aside for the discussion of spiritual issues or the teaching of meditation exercises, or even regular meditation periods in the timetable. While Buber believed that the education of character 'is not achieved through the direct teaching of ethics', he nevertheless admitted that it will involve some reflection upon ethics (Smith, 2000, n.p.). What must be resisted is the temptation of the complacent assumption that, as Farrell puts it in relation to the problem of moral education, 'our attempts to "educate" (in this case within the moral domain) within the constraints and rituals of formal schooling will somehow produce (or at least can produce, if properly planned and organized) "moral learning" among the subjects of our schooling enterprise' (2003, p. 113). As Erricker observes:

> in the social sphere there always exists a political and economic climate within which relations work and of which those relations are themselves an expression … Once this is understood we cannot pretend that our ability to relate to one another can be approached educationally without attention being paid to the political climate framing and suffusing relations. To do so would be to create a code of values that breaks down every time it is challenged by that climate, i.e. once there is a politico-social price to pay. Thus, there is a lip service paid to 'warmth', as far as values and relations are concerned, which, since it has no political context, disappears when that political climate changes. Educationally,therefore, the climate is not mentioned. The values are preached or explored in the sterile and irrelevant isolation of the classroom without reference to the social reality in which they are to be employed. (2002, pp. 40–1)

Discrete elements of the spiritual education curriculum work and are made sense of in the context of the overall school and even social ethos, rather than achieve their effect in isolation of this context. A well-intentioned initiative, when carried out against the background of a surrounding hidden curriculum of contrary purposes, will either serve to subvert that hidden curriculum, particularly if the hidden curriculum is explicitly exposed, recognized and critiqued, or be itself subverted by the hidden curriculum, particularly if the latter is unchallenged or seen to be unchallengeable, even contributing to more cynicism. Thus we should always proceed cautiously and not take things at their face value. Another feature of compartmentalized spiritual education initiatives that likely compromises their effectiveness is the compartmentalization itself, which supports a model of the human person as an aggregate of discrete knowledge, skills and attributes that can be assembled together like a factory product, a model that subtly conveys an expectation to pupils of what they are like and how they deserve to be treated that is contradictory to the spiritual understanding of human beings. And this reminds us that the adjective spiritual in the term 'spiritual education' should properly describe the nature rather than only the 'content' and 'intended outcome' of that education. An education in spirituality should itself be spiritual. This is different from the case of, say, geography education, where it makes little sense to describe the education as geographical.

The non-linear dynamics of the spirit

In its essence, the idea that education in spirituality should itself be spiritual is similar to the view that effective spiritual education is, first and foremost, rendered by the social ethos. And they both contain within themselves a paradox that should lead us to rethink their soundness, or at least harbour some reservation about them. This is similar to the Socratic paradox of how on earth it is possible for anyone to learn anything, or, for that matter, for anyone to teach anything to another. To be able to learn anything new, one has to be already in possession of the requisite knowledge about the thing to be learned that is necessary for comprehending and assimilating the new knowledge. Hence it is impossible to learn anything radically new; all learning is nothing other than recollection. Analogously, since education in spirituality must itself be spiritual, there is no way in which spirituality can arise or be cultivated if the social ethos is spiritually toxic. There is simply no point through which the spirit can enter this closed circle. And this seems to be borne out by the fact that, despite the unending flow of critiques of the corrosive effects on human character and spirituality ever since the advent of industrialization and urbanization, to such an extent that they now sound mere platitudes, such critiques have not succeeded in stemming the tide. Despite pockets of resistance in such forms as alternative communities and the counter-culture, the overall trend towards industrialization (and its putative successor post-industrialization) and urbanization continues to accelerate, and the evolving social forms into which we find ourselves moving do not seem less malignant than their predecessors. There is no shortage of memes flowing around that protest the suffocating of the spirit, but they do not constitute the dominant discourse, and industrialization and urbanization, and now technologization and globalization, seem just to follow their own inexorable developmental dynamics like that of a cancer growth. Yes, there is room for the more or less free flow of these dissenting memes— and this is something we must be thankful for—but they do not seem to matter much.

Yet the idea that spiritual education is impossible under current social conditions is, of course, contrary to our understanding of the nature of spirit and spirituality: recall that 'it is a characteristic of spirit and the spiritual that it is dynamic' (Priestley, 1985, p. 114). It breaks out in unexpected moments and places. If we do take the ideas of spirituality and spiritual education seriously, we should not give up on the possibility of achieving something meaningful through less than perfect means, such as meditation classes and discussions of spiritual issues, under less than ideal conditions, and should try to do as much as we can, even as we uphold in principle the ideas that education in spirituality should itself be spiritual and that effective spiritual education is firstly rendered by the social ethos. For one thing, the fact that the proliferation of dissenting memes and subversive initiatives has so far produced no significant effect in stemming the onslaught of forces that make our social environment toxic does not mean that the growth of these memes and practices does not actually matter. We cannot tell in advance when their growth approaches the critical mass requiring only a last straw to tip the scale and reverse or put right the trend, the point at which the spirit breaks open and enters the circle. There may indeed be a dynamic governing all this, but that of non-linear dynamics. In mathematical jargon, 'after the 1 catastrophe [the sudden, huge change that is initiated when the critical mass is 2 reached] then you may end up on an attractor [a stable state, such as a new social 3 ethos] that you never knew existed [you never knew was possible]'[5] (Cohen & Stewart, 1994, p. 211). Gladwell, the writer who popularized the concept of the 'tipping point' with his bestseller of the same title, puts the same point in less intimidating language: in social epidemics 'change happens not gradually but at one dramatic moment' (Gladwell, 2000, p. 9). He advises that: 'What must underlie successful epidemics [roughly meaning "social movement" in this context], in the end, is a bedrock belief that change is possible, that people can radically transform their behaviour or beliefs in the face of the right kind of impetus' (p. 258). Those who are concerned with spiritual education would do well to heed this piece of sagely advice (or platitude, which is probably the same thing).

Bootstrapping spiritual education

Furthermore, there is the argument that features of human character, such as virtue and spirituality, can be cultivated through the pursuit of practices that are initially not completely or properly virtuous or spiritual. At first glance, this view seems to contradict the idea that education in spirituality must itself be spiritual, but in fact the two need not be contradictory, at least not entirely so, as I hope to show in due course. Take the example of language learning. Whereas the possibility cannot be ruled out that, occasionally, an infant might happen to have formed a certain concept in its mind before being taught or discovering its verbal label, thereby learning the word and grasping its meaning, in the majority of cases, an infant just gets immersed in a language environment before there are even vaguely formed concepts in its mind. In the course of language learning, infants are bombarded with pieces of language in the context of real-world interactions. Through initially 'senseless' sound play in imitation of the language pieces they hear or in response to encouragement by adults, or in myriad other ways, they somehow suddenly grasp the meaning of the initially senseless sound-complex and hence the idea or concept it signified.

A moving example of this process is provided by Helen Keller, who told the story of how the persevering effort of her dedicated teacher finally enabled her to grasp the meaning of the word 'water', the first word she was ever able to make sense of, and the enlightening effect this first discovery had on her. This is a mysterious process: meaning arising or emerging out of the engagement in pre-semantic behaviour. However, note that certain conditions must be satisfied for this mysterious process to work. The child must be engaged to and by the language community in active interaction. An infant watching television alone, though heavily bombarded with pieces of verbal language, will never learn the language and be thus enabled to grasp the concepts these pieces of language signify.

What all this discussion of the discovery of meaning and hence the cultivation of the intellect initially through the play or practice of not-yet understood language is intended to suggest is that the cultivation of virtue and spirituality can, if not must, follow an analogous path. Comte-Sponville explains the process of becoming virtuous by quoting the great philosophers:

> There are no natural virtues; hence we must become virtuous. How? 'For the things we have to learn before we can do them', Aristotle explains, 'we learn by doing them.' Yet how can we do them if we haven't learned them? … 'We become just', Aristotle continues, 'by doing just acts, temperate by doing temperate acts, brave by doing brave acts'. But can we act justly without being just? Temperately without being temperate? Bravely without being brave? And if we cannot, then how do we become just, temperate, brave? (2001, pp.10–11)

That paradox is analogous to the Socratic paradox about the (im)possibility of learning. Comte-Sponville invokes Kant for a solution to this paradox:

> For him [Kant], these first semblances of virtue can be explained in terms of discipline, in other words, as a product of external constraint: what the child cannot do on his own because he has no instinct of it 'others have to do … for him', and in this way 'one gener- ation educates the next'. It is by mimicking the ways of virtue … that we stand a chance of becoming virtuous … If we can become moral (and for morality even to be possible—and immorality, too, for that matter—it must be the case that we can), it is not through virtue but through education, not for goodness' sake but for form's sake, not for moral reasons but for reasons of politeness. Morality is first artifice, then artifact. By imitating virtue we become virtuous. 'For when men play these roles', writes Kant, 'virtues are gradually established, whose appearance had up until now only been affected. These virtues ultimately will become part of the actor's disposition'. (2001, pp.11–12)

What Comte-Sponville seems to be saying is that an initially hollow, external behavioural form, when deployed often enough, will give rise to the inner substance of character it is supposed to express. This view might be termed an 'emergence' model of virtue development. Here the term 'emergence' alludes to the philosophical idea that reality is a multi-levelled structure, with a higher level of reality being the emergent property of the entities one level below, when these entities are organized in the proper manner. A more sophisticated version of this model of reality posits bi-directional inter-level influences, in the sense that the entities on a certain level not only give rise to a higher, emergent level of reality, but are themselves influenced or conditioned by the higher-level qualities they have given rise to, and, in turn, influence or condition the lower-level entities that have given rise to them. For example, one attempt to solve the age-old mind–body puzzle suggests that the behaviour and interactions of brain cells properly configured give rise to the emergent property of consciousness, the operation of which, in turn, in some way influences or conditions the operations of the brain. The emergence model of virtue development then proposes that actions and practices that are imitations of virtuous actions and practices, when engaged in often enough, will somehow give rise to the imitated virtue as an emergent, higher-level feature of the individual who engages in such actions and practices.

I would suggest that the range of application of the 'emergence model' can be extended beyond virtue development to also cover language development and spiritual development, and possibly other phenomena too. In the case of language, the frequent pre-semantic deployment of language forms (behaviour) will give rise to a grasp of the meaning signified by these forms (cognition). True to the bi-directional nature of inter-level interaction, once the child grasps the meanings signified by the language forms, his use of these language forms will change, in the sense that it will now be informed by the meaning the child wishes to express. In the case of spiritual development, the regular engagement in spiritual practices will enhance one's spirituality as an attribute of one's inner being.

The educative role of the community

In what sense does this not contradict the view that education in spirituality must itself be spiritual? I will argue that in fact not all engagement in spiritual practices will contribute to enhancing one's spirituality. Recall that in the case of language learning,the child must be engaged to and by the language community in active interaction,otherwise no amount of passive immersion in the language will lead to any break- through to understanding.[6] Similarly, the mere mechanical performance of a spiritual practice, in a community that does not take the practice seriously, is likely to contribute to alienation rather than spiritual development. At best the child can only learn to engage in the spiritual practice in the same spiritless, if not hypocritical, way as those adults around him do. Confucius was well aware of this danger:

> The Master said, A man who is not Good,7 what can he have to do with ritual? A man who is not Good, what can he have to do with music? (Confucius,2000, p.86)
>
> The Master said, Ritual, ritual! Does it mean no more than presents of jade and silk? Music, music! Does it mean no more than bells and drums? (p.201)

Of course, at the outset, a novice can only simulate a virtuous action or spiritual practice. However, the unit of analysis should be larger than the individual novice,just as in language learning, the unit of analysis is the infant and its social circle. In the absence of the support of a social circle, an infant imitating TV sounds will never learn any language. Now argument by analogy is shaky, and I do not rule out the possibility that the mere 'going through the motions' of a spiritual practice such as, say, meditation may produce a spiritual experience in the form of a heightened state of consciousness. This would be particularly likely in the case either of a spiritual genius, or of someone who treats the practice very seriously. However, I believe that the case of language learning can throw important light on how spiritual education is possible and how it is impeded in many cases. A novice can indeed only simulate the form of spiritual practices. However, if the models from whom he copies the form are themselves serious about the spiritual practices, that is their spiritual practices are indeed expressions of the inner spirituality of their character, the inner spirituality of the novice will be ignited through the catalyst of the practice of the form. On the other hand, to take an extreme, hypothetical case, if the teachers of spiritual education are themselves hypocrites, who discuss spiritual issues with pupils because that is prescribed in the school curriculum, but are otherwise uninterested in these spiritual issues, their hypocrisy cannot but be detected by the pupils, resulting in more spiritual harm than good. In this sense, the success of the spiritual education of the common people still depends to a large extent on a spiritual social ethos.

In conclusion, we should heed the advice of the ancient sages to avoid extreme positions.[8] A strong spiritual ethos is not an absolute necessity for spiritual education to be possible, but nor is spiritual education easily realized *ex nihilo* irrespective of the social context. On balance, I believe that, in the absence of a strong spiritual social ethos, spiritual education, though not impossible, will face serious impediments. Trying to transcend these impediments to our pursuit of spiritual education is a way for us to realize our nature as spiritual beings.

Notes

1. This last phrase is a very rough formulation. There is a sense in which one's committed goal is constitutive of one's (expanded) self. The self grows by transcending itself. Perhaps a better formulation would be 'goals that go beyond the egoistic self', but 'egoistic' might sound redundant as an adjective of 'self', and anyway begs further explication.
2. Jung sometimes describes the collective unconscious as the product of the evolutionary heritage of the human species, evident in such phenomena as archetypes and universal dream symbolism. In this sense, the collective unconscious is not necessarily a spiritual realm. However, in many other instances, such as in discussions of the phenomenon of 'synchronicity', the collective unconscious as construed by Jung is something that is a properly 'transpersonal' realm that hovers over, or underlies, all individual human beings, constituting a medium through which the separation of individuals can be transcended.
3. I admit that I may be mistaken on this point. For example, value is directly grasped in a 'value sensing' type of raised awareness, which means that there is a self-contained, holistic perception of the value, its significance and its justifications, if such distinctions are meaningful at all in relation to the experience. The experience itself is the justification for the perceived value. Therefore there may not be any subsequent need to account for the perceived value separately. Still, analytically the ontological status of the source of the value is an issue, only that probably the answer to this is already included in the value sensing perception itself.
4. 'Goodness' is the sinologist Arthur Waley's rendition of the fundamental Confucian concept of ren, which has been given different translations by different authors. For example, Fung (1997) translated it as 'human-heartedness'.
5. The following fuller quote reinforces the point about the unpredictable character of the future, a future that cannot be assumed simply by extrapolating current trends: 'after the catastrophe you may end up on an attractor that you never knew existed. It was busy developing, out in the mathematical space of the possible, but you didn't notice it because the new attractor wasn't being physically expressed. Suddenly it is expressed, and the mathematical fiction gobbles up your own reality and lands you in totally unexpected circumstances' (Cohen & Stewart, 1994, p. 211).
6. In other words, the child learns the language as it is used by those around it to communicate among themselves and, more importantly, to interact with it in a meaningful way. In this sense, the community and the child born into it are totally committed to the language. This commitment on the part of the community of which the child is a member is crucial.
7. 'Good' is Arthur Waley's translation for ren, which has often been alternatively rendered as 'human-hearted'; see n.4, above.
8. This is, of course, a simplified and distorted formulation for the sake of ease of expression. This advice should not be taken as itself advocating an extreme position of avoiding extreme positions in all cases and at all costs. Instead it recommends giving everything its proper due, no more and no less.

References

Anderson, M. L. & Taylor, H. F. (2000) *Sociology: understanding a diverse society* (Belmont, CA, Wadsworth/Thomson Learning).

Bateson, M. C. (2000) *Full circles, overlapping lives: culture and generation in transition* (New York, Random House).

Clinton, H. R. (1996) *It takes a village: and other lessons children teach us* (New York, Simon & Schuster).

Cohen, J. & Stewart, I. (1994) *The collapse of chaos: discovering simplicity in a complex world* (New York, Penguin).

Comte-Sponville, A. (2001) *A small treatise on the great virtues: the uses of philosophy in everyday life* (Catherine Temerson, Trans.) (New York, Metropolitan Books).

Confucius (2000) *The analects* (Arthur Waley, Trans.) (London, Everyman).

Emmons, R. A. (1999) *The psychology of ultimate concerns: motivation and spirituality in personality* (New York, The Guilford Press).

Erricker, C. (2002) *When learning becomes your enemy: the relationship between education, spiritual dissent and economics* (Nottingham, Educational Heretics Press).

Farrell, J. P. (2003) 'Hey Joe ...' Moral education, moral learning, and how could we ever know if and when the first produces the second? *Curriculum Inquiry*, 33(2), 105–115.

Fung, Y. L. (1997) *A short history of Chinese philosophy: a systematic account of Chinese thought from its origins to the present day* (Derk Bodde, Ed.) (New York, The Free Press).

Garbarino, J. (1995) Growing up in a socially toxic environment: life for children and families in the 1990s, in: G. B. Melton (Ed.) *The individual, the family, and social good: personal fulfillment in times of change* (Lincoln, NB, University of Nebraska Press), 1–20.

Gladwell, M. (2000) *Tipping point: how little things can make a big difference* (Boston, MA, Little, Brown).

Hart, T. (2003) *The secret spiritual world of children* (Makawao, HI, Inner Ocean).

Hay, D. (1995) The validity of the experiential approach to religious education, *Hong Kong Journal of Religious Education*, 7(1), 14–26.

Hay, D. with Nye, R. (1998) *The spirit of the child* (London, HarperCollins Religious).

Horgan, J. (2003) *Rational mysticism: dispatches from the border between science and spirituality* (New York, NY, Houghton Mifflin).

Priestley, J. G. (1985) Towards finding the hidden curriculum: a consideration of the spiritual dimension of experience in curriculum planning, *British Journal of Religious Education*, 7(3), 112–119.

Smith, M. K. (2000) Martin Buber on education, in: *The encyclopedia of informal education*. Available online at: http://www.infed.org/thinders/et-buber.htm (accessed 13 July 2004).

Thich, N. H. (1997) The sun my heart, in: A. Kotler (Ed.) *Engaged Buddhist reader: ten years of engaged Buddhist publishing* (Berkeley, CA, Parallax Press), 162–170.

Wang, R. R. (2003) *Images of women in Chinese thought and culture* (Indianapolis, IN, Hackett)

Yaron, K. (1993) Martin Buber, *Prospects: the quarterly review of comparative education*, 23(1–2), 135–46. Available online at: http://www.unesco.org/International/Publications/Thinkers/ThinkersPdf/bubere.pdf (accessed 13 July 2004).

The empathetic mind: the essence of human spirituality

Marian de Souza

ABSTRACT
The discovery of mirror neurons has led to some exciting research into the role of the brain and human empathy. Empathy is a significant element in human relationality and, therefore, human spirituality. This article will focus on the links between mirror neurons and human empathy and education. It will then examine how technology may be a factor in causing the erosion of empathy in today's world, leading to school violence and bullying. It will conclude by offering some guidelines for educational programmes which may lead to the nurturing of children's empathy.

In the mid-nineties, many Year 12 students in Catholic schools claimed to be spiritual but not religious and this triggered my research into spirituality. It was important to understand exactly what they meant. The subsequent research journey led to many different disciplines and networks of academics, professionals and practitioners, who had all been investigating contemporary spirituality. It is clear that, in the western world, where spirituality was once aligned and often confused with religion and religiosity, it is now the subject of discussion in so many different fields that encompass aspects of human learning and living. Nonetheless, the disputed notion that spirituality cannot be defined continues so that it remains a hazy, vague, contested concept and the accompanying research can become tainted with such ambiguity. For many religionists and theologians, spirituality is about the human person's relationship with a Supreme Being – known as God or by various names and in different forms in different faith traditions. From this perspective, spirituality becomes something learned or a gift given to a chosen people and so on. However, in the contemporary world, there are a large number of individuals who identify themselves as people who do not believe in a God or a Divine Consciousness/Energy and if we examine spiritual characteristics such as truth, justice, beauty, freedom, caring, joyfulness, mystery, awe, wonder, empathy and compassion, we find these traits in many non-religious people. So my research followed on from others where spirituality was viewed as an innate human trait which may not be confined to the religious dimensions of human life or indeed, restricted to an understanding that it reflects a relationship with God.1 Instead, human spirituality may be perceived as a raised awareness/consciousness of oneself as a relational Being, that is, an awareness that Self is part of the Whole which also comprises Other. The end point in human spiritual growth reaches a realm of Ultimate Unity2 where the individual may be said to have reached a level of consciousness or awareness that has sometimes been referred to as Unity Consciousness (Wilber 1999, 440)3 or Supermind (Ghose cited in Maitra 2000, 56)4 or Cosmic Consciousness (Bucke 1905).

This understanding of spirituality as pertaining to the relational dimension of being human has some relevance for this article since the discovery of mirror neurons provide physical evidence that something happens in our brain which may mirror another's emotions and/or actions and therefore, may have implications for human spirituality in terms of connectedness and/or relationality.

This article, then, examines some of the findings in neuroscience that relate to mirror neurons and the implications for spirituality in terms of a sense of connectedness. It will also focus on the concept of empathy and how empathy may be eroded through the excessive use of technology in the lives of children and young people today. The erosion of empathy can lead to school violence and bullying which is a factor that has raised deep concerns for parents, educators and other professionals who work with children and young people. Finally, drawing on the discussion presented in this article, guidelines are offered for the development of learning programmes and environments that will help to nurture the empathetic dimension of children's lives which, potentially, should improve their spiritual well-being.

Mirror neurons and human spirituality (Connectedness. Reaching out and reaching in. Empathy)

Mirror neurons were discovered by an Italian neuroscientist Rizzolati and his team in the 1990s. Needless to say, much of the literature about mirror neurons does not make any references to human spirituality. The focus has been more on their use in clinical work with patients displaying neurological disorders. However, recent studies (Iacoboni 2008; Rizzolatti and Sinigaglia 2008; Keysers 2011) suggest that when we are confronted with another person's distress and we find ourselves saying, 'I really do feel your hurt or anger', neurologically speaking, we actually are equipped to do just that. Iacaboni contends that we react to a movie character's distress, chivalry and so on, precisely because the mirror neurons in our brains re-create for us whatever we are actually watching, 'We have empathy for the fictional characters – we know how they're feeling – because we literally experience the same feelings ourselves' (4). He extends this discussion to claim:

> 'Vicarious' is not a strong enough word to describe the effect of these mirror neurons. When we see someone else suffering or in pain, mirror neurons help us to read her or his facial expression and actually make us feel the suffering or the pain of the other person. These moments, I will argue, are the foundation of empathy and possibly of morality, a morality that is deeply rooted in our biology. (5)

Iacoboni (2008) cites Vittorio Gallese, who was part of Rizzolatti's original team and who also had an interest in philosophy, as the first person to propose a role of mirror neurons in both understanding and empathising with the emotions of other people (108) and claims that, today, there is much empirical evidence to suggest a strong link between mirror neurons and empathy:

> This evidence has been gathered using different methodologies in neuroscience, from brain imaging to the study of brain-damaged patients, even looking at the data from depth electrodes implanted in neuro-surgical patients. (109)

The eminent neuroscientist, Ramachandran (2011) observes that the significance of mirror neurons is that they are not just motor-command neurons because they appear to have predictive power, that is, they allow a person to read another's mind and s/ he can figure out what the other person is about to do, as if 'mirror neurons are nature's own virtual–reality simulations of the intentions of other beings' (121). Expounding this notion, Ramachandran refers to experiments which indicate the ability of these cells to empathise with others and likes to call them 'Gandhi neurons' because they 'blur the boundary between self and others' (124). He notes that this could become a problem if there was nothing to prevent individuals from blindly imitating every action they see or literally feeling someone else's pain. He speculates that there may be a frontal inhibitory circuit that suppresses the automatic mimicry when it is inappropriate. This theory is supported by research by both Iacoboni (2008) and Keysers (2011). Ramachandran concludes that:

> It is the dynamic interplay of signals from frontal inhibitory circuits, mirror neurons (both frontal and parietal), and null signals from receptors that allow you to enjoy reciprocity with others while simultaneously preserving your individuality.

Expanding on this theory, Ramachandran (2011) discusses the human characteristic to be introspective and to have self-awareness. He argues that it is possible that mirror neurons turn inwards to enable a representation of one's own mind: 'With the mirror-neuron system thus "bent back" on itself full-circle, self-awareness was born' (260) Know thyself.

> 'Science tells us we are merely beasts, but we don't feel like that. We feel like angels trapped inside the bodies of beasts, forever craving transcendence'. That's the essential human predicament in a nutshell. (Ramachandran 2011, 291)

Ramachandran further argues that other-awareness and self-awareness 'co-evolved, enriching each other enormously and culminating in the kind of reciprocity between self-awareness and other-awareness seen only in humans' (260).

Other research suggests there are different types of mirror neurons. Apart from the visual mirror neurons which allow the individual to see another person's visual and conceptual stance (Ramachandran 2011) there are also auditory mirror neurons (Keysers 2011) and sensory mirror neurons (Keysers 2011; Ramachandran 2011).

Keysers (2011) recent research has confirmed the notion that other people's emotions become our emotions almost as if what is happening to others actually envelops us: 'Experiencing this doesn't even take effort. We just do it, automatically, intuitively, and largely uncontrollably' (8) and he further claims that this 'feat of our brains, the emotional connection with others is, to a large extent, what makes us human' (8) without which our social lives and social networks would break down since the success of our personal and professional relationships depends on our ability to read the emotional states of others, including when they may try to hide an inner turmoil that is devouring them. Keysers contends that: 'Mirror neurons "mirror" the behaviour and emotions of the people surrounding us in such a way that the others become part of us' (10).

As with most ideas in the human world, there are differing views about the role of mirror neurons in generating empathy. Dossey (2010), questions whether mirror neurons can explain the 'conscious experience of empathy or any other complex social emotion' (106). He argues that the neuroscientists may have it backwards and that we don't know if it is mirror neurons that send empathic messages to conscious awareness but that, in fact, it may be 'the felt experience of empathy that causes the empathy neurons to light up' (107). Citing Sperry's (1966) discussion of downward causation to support his stance, Dossey states:

> Any model or description [of the brain] that leaves out conscious forces ... is bound to be sadly incomplete and unsatisfactory ... This scheme [downward causation] is one that puts mind back over matter, in a sense, not under or outside or beside it. It is a scheme that idealizes ideas and ideals over physical and chemical interactions, nerve impulse traffic and DNA. (cited in Dossey 2010, 107)

Nonetheless, Dossey does not deny that empathy is an essential human experience and in his final estimate, he reflects that:

> The main contribution of the mirror-neuron hypothesis is that it is a partial corrective to the view that we humans are overwhelmingly selfish creatures whose sole evolutionary imperative is to survive, reproduce, and perpetuate our genes, at whatever cost to those outside our kinship group. The mirror-neuron hypothesis suggest that we are equipped for empathy, compassion, altruism, and cooperation, in addition to being biologically geared for competition, procreation and survival. (116)

However, the purpose of this paper is not to examine the different perspectives about the role of mind, consciousness and the brain nor does it aim to present an extensive discussion on mirror neurons. Rather, it merely intends to explore a particular perspective: that it is possible that mirror neurons provide physical evidence that the human person is wired to be empathetic. Empathy is absolutely foundational to successful human relationships and, if connectedness expressed through relationality is the essence of human spirituality, empathy then becomes the experience and expression of spirituality and, accordingly, a distinguishing human trait.

Empathy

As different cultures, religions and worldviews have become next door neighbours in a contemporary global world, there has been much lack of understanding and suspicion of Other and it may have been the triggering factor for the reason why empathy and compassion have become words that have appeared with greater frequency in this past decade than in the last 20 years of the twentieth Century. In Baron-Cohen's (2011) extensive treatise on empathy, he identified two aspects to empathy: recognition and response.

> empathy is our ability to identify what someone else is thinking or feeling, and to respond to their thoughts and feelings with an appropriate emotion.

Baron-Cohen also proposed an empathy continuum with zero degrees at one end. The atrocities that frequently comprise our daily news are usually committed by people who reflect zero degrees of empathy. Their feelings for Other border on the non-existent so that their persons and their lives are not affected by the distress and/or the calamity they cause. In the case of most individuals, the level of empathy may vary depending on their circumstances and/or emotional states, so that they may move up and down the continuum but for some individuals, their empathy remains quite stable at zero degrees. Baron-Cohen argues that when empathy is suspended, the individual has 'single-minded attention' which means that they are thinking only of their own interests, within their own mind are current thoughts or perceptions. 'Double-minded' attention means that we are keeping in mind someone else's mind, at the very same time.5 (Baron-Cohen 2011, 10).

I would suggest that there is a distinct alignment between the relational continuum proposed for human spirituality (de Souza 2012) and Baron-Cohen's empathy continuum. Recognition of the connectedness that the individual experiences to other underpins the concept of both continua, and accompanying this is the recognition that actions and behaviour correspond to where the individual stands on each continuum.

The erosion of empathy

Arguably, babies are born into this world deeply connected to everything around them and it is through the socialisation process that they become disconnected. Their openness to Other, their sense of freedom, curiosity and adventurous spirit is often stifled in our efforts to protect them and make them conform to the expectations of the society in which we live. By the time they are a few years old, their identities have already been shaped by the culture of compartmentalisation: they become, for different periods of time, a member of a family, playgroup, classroom, sporting team and so on and they learn appropriate behaviour for each of these identities. As they end primary school and begin secondary school, around the age of 12, their identities continue to be shaped by the latest communication gadget or software – mobile phones, i-pads, Facebook, MySpace, Instagram and so on.6 For many, their sense of Self, then, becomes dependent on their popularity and status amongst their peers and it become important to have a large network of friends on Facebook, or to whom they can text, tweet and so on. There is a downside to this kind of social networking because it does make our experiences of connectedness a 'distant connectedness' (de Souza 2009) or what Turkle (2011) calls being 'alone together'.7 And it also allows a certain amount of anonymity where one can create a desirable persona, but which is a step or two removed from the 'real me'.

Technology may also provide a child with a safe haven. If their world is not a safe and happy place, children may retreat into the excitement of a virtual world where they are in control and where they can create new identities through which they can play out all their desires and aspirations. Not surprisingly, when they are 'unplugged' from this virtual world, their real world may become a boring and often, insecure place, one from which they may mentally and emotionally retreat so that they become more and more isolated. The ability to create online persona for themselves may also cause individuals to lose their connectedness to their real Self, the inner person. This is more than likely to cause underlying anxiety and tension in the lives of individuals as they lose sight of the person they are meant to be or, indeed, a sense of disappointment because they feel they are not the person they want to be! Turkle puts this succinctly:

> As we distribute ourselves, we may abandon ourselves ... In all of this, there is a nagging question: Does virtual intimacy degrade our experience of the other kind and, indeed, of all encounters, of any kind? (12)

Certainly, as humans, we are physical beings and it is through our senses that we engage with others to establish and maintain relationships. Through seeing, hearing, speaking to and touching another, a particularly human dimension of communication is created. Our physical senses are important elements in helping us understand and truly communicate with another and mirror neurons have an important role in this process. Many studies cited by Iacoboni indicate that, 'through imitation and mimicry we are able to feel what other people feel. By being able to feel what others feel, we are also able to respond compassionately to their emotional states' (Iacoboni

2008, 114). However, when we communicate through a technological device, such as mobile phones and the internet, the intimacy generated through our physical senses and which is important and enriching to human relationships may be lost. The distant connectedness impedes our ability to 'read' another's face or really hear the emotions in another's voice. Certainly we are unable to reach out and physically hug another in an act of comfort. Thus, the distant connectedness engendered through the process of communicating through technology promotes the possibilities for 'dehumanization and objectification that are present when the "zone of intimacy" becomes a line before which is "we" and beyond which is "them"' (Hess 2012, citing Hundeide, 412).

It would seem, then, that technological forms of communication have allowed bullies to invent and access new ways of reaching their victims in a particularly sinister and menacing manner. The perpetrators are not only able to reside in anonymity, thereby reducing the chances of being outed and having to face up to their victims but they also do not physically witness, at the moment of impact, the distress they have caused which would be expressed on the victim's face or through the emotional turmoil in the victim's voice. In other words, the 'distant connectedness' (de Souza 2009) implicit in technological communications do not allow mirror neurons from being activated for simulated facial feedback. Iacoboni (2008) claims that 'This simulation process is not an effortful, deliberate pretence of being in somebody else's shoes. It is an effortless, automatic, and unconscious inner mirroring' (120). This could mean that a cyberbully's mirror neurons may not trigger a spontaneous, empathetic response precisely because s/he cannot physically see her/ his victim.

Yet, another aspect that needs to be considered is that the imitative action of mirror neurons may relate to the increased violence in schools and in societies. Iacoboni (2008) cites research that suggests that if children watch a short violent movie it will result in imitative violence amongst them:

> A consistent finding is typically observed in these experiments. The children who watched the violent short movies display much more aggressive subsequent behaviour toward both people and objects than the children who watched nonviolent short movies. The effect of media violence on imitative violence is observed in children from preschool to adolescence, in both boys and girls, in both naturally aggressive and nonaggressive children, and in different races. (206)

He goes on to examine the real-life impact of media violence on people's (including older people's) actual conduct in the world and concludes:

> Children who watch more media violence tend to be more aggressive than other children. These finding are highly reproducible across studies and even across countries. Pairing the

> findings from the correlational studies with the findings from the laboratory experiments with children does tempt us to conclude that media violence inspires imitative violence. (207)

He concedes that the most reliable empirical data about the impact of media violence must come from longitudinal studies that investigate the correlation between watching media violence and violent behaviour over time. He makes a reference to a few such studies and offers the following conclusion:

> Taken together, the findings from laboratory studies, correlational studies, and longitudinal studies all support the hypothesis that media violence induces imitative violence. In fact, the statistical 'effect size' – a measure of the strength of the relationship between two variables – for media violence and aggression far exceeds the effect sizes of passive smoking and lung cancer, or calcium intake and bone mass, or asbestos exposure and cancer. (208–209)

Iacoboni acknowledges that these findings have been met with some scepticism in the past but argues that the discovery of mirror neurons has changed this since it further informs our understanding about the hows and whys of imitative violence in the human world. These new understandings of imitative violence have enormous significance for both society and education. However, as Iacoboni reflects, with a powerful media and an economy driven culture, ridding society of screen violence is not going to happen any time soon. Instead, educators, have once again to find a way to deal with the problems generated at the wider societal level.

Mirror neurons and the implications for education

The problem: bullying and school violence

A very real problem for schools in Australia and elsewhere is the case of bullying and violence, and the first element of Baron-Cohen's definition of empathy has relevance here. For instance, cyberbullies act furtively and therefore have no opportunity to physically recognise the distress of their victims as shown through face and body. Thus, the first element of empathy is missing and, logically then, the second element of empathy cannot follow. This is not to say that all cyberbullies stay at zero degrees of empathy on the empathy continuum. At times they may be much higher up the continuum and feel some empathy for some people in their world. However, at the moments during their bullying actions, their empathy levels would appear to have been suspended.

Generally, bullies and those prone to violence objectify their victims thereby dismissing their value and feelings as individuals. They clearly display the 'single-minded attention' rather than the 'double minded attention' as discussed by Baron-Cohen (2011, 10). Their own interests and goals become all encompassing and there is little or no empathic recognition of Other. Their empathy has been eroded (Baron-Cohen 2011, 4). This appears to reflect Buber's I–It relationship since the relation to Thou is direct:

> The primary word I-Thou can be spoken only with the whole being. Concentration and fusion into the whole being can never take place through my agency, nor can it ever take place without me. I become through my relation to Thou; as I become I, I say Thou. All real living is meeting. (see Glatzer 1966, 48)

Without empathy, children and young people have difficulty relating to others and this can lead to them craving attention or trying to dominate others, both of which are identifiable traits of a bully. Accordingly, raising the awareness of children and young people that they are spiritual beings whose essence is connectedness to everything other than Self may be a promising starting point in intervention programmes to prevent school violence and bullying. With the knowledge we have of the imitative action of mirror neurons, it is possible to develop activities to promote empathy amongst school kids.

Implications for addressing the spiritual dimension in learning: nurturing empathy

If the existence of difference has the potential to be a triggering factor in bullying amongst children, a proactive response would be to focus on educational programmes which help promote children's awareness that they are relational beings; that they are connected to Other. In this respect, mirror neurons have a distinct role to play since experiences of connectedness are more likely to promote feelings of empathy towards the Other. Such programmes would have significant value in multicultural and multi-religious societies where connectedness and empathy need to be foundational factors in order to promote social cohesion and the well-being of both community and individual. In order to do this, school curricula need to explore alternative ways to promote knowledge by recognising the imitative action of mirror neurons in the learning process. For instance, they should:

- Recognise and address the impact of mirror neurons on the relational aspect of students' lives in terms of the connectedness they experience and express since relationality is a vital ingredient in their spiritual, emotional and, therefore, their intellectual and physical well-being.
- Develop inclusive communities where time and space is provided to share stories. When listening to another's story we often experience a sense of connection since their story may resonate with our own stories. As well, these experiences create opportunities for individuals to 'mirror' or imitate the action and experience from someone else's story, thereby, forging previously unknown and unrealised associations. Further, they offer a chance for students to discover 'the Other' within themselves.
- Welcome and celebrate diversity in a real and meaningful way, whereby, the imitative action of mirror neurons may help children to recognise similarities amidst differences which may, in turn, engender a genuine sense of belonging.
- Offer opportunities for students to develop their empathy through creative and imaginative activities and thinking within and outside their usual framework.
- Appreciate the role of the arts in the enhancement and expression of individual and communal empathy through the action of mirror neurons in eliciting the individual's response through the different physical senses. As Robinson (2013) identifies: 'Arts are important, not because they improve Maths scores but because they speak to parts of children's Being which is otherwise untouched' (the emphasis is mine).
- Encourage an imitative response through role modelling when teaching students to accept responsibility and commit to action for the common good.

Teachers should be conscious that mirror neurons have an impact on their own sense of connectedness to and empathy for Other which may help them:

- recognise and nurture experiences of connectedness in their students;
- continue to be consistent, empathetic and non-judgemental in the care they extend to their students;
- value the plurality and diversity amongst their students and recognise how to use this feature effectively to enhance an empathic learning environment;
- remain vigilant and retain high levels of awareness of Other so as not to become complacent about their own ability to be inclusive;
- acknowledge that the rapid pace of change, driven by technology, may cause anxiety, restlessness, discomfort and instability both for themselves and their students and it requires an appropriate and considered response.

It is important that educators utilise and empathise with the rich heritage and wisdom of different traditions and cultures that compose the pluralistic, globalised world and which are so often evident in local, contemporary classrooms. By providing opportunities for students to explore, through shared stories, experiences and vision, the mystery and wonder that accompany the search for meaning by people from varied backgrounds, teachers can engage the rational, physical, emotional and spiritual dimensions of learning. If students through the action of their mirror neurons discover that their stories resonate with others, this will, potentially, raise their awareness of their connectedness with Other which, in turn, should promote a feeling of empathy and enhance the spiritual dimension of learning. These are just some of the factors that point to the need for new learning structures and spaces and for programmes to be embedded in whole new frameworks which are more meaningful and relevant to the lives of young people today and which may help them develop into active, thoughtful and empathetic citizens in their future communities.

Notes

1. While I have several publications that have touched on this over the past decade, a very recent one in which I explain in much greater detail than before is the following article: de Souza (2012). Connectedness and Connectedness. The dark side of spirituality: Implications for education. *International Journal of children's Spirituality* 17 (3): 291–304.
2. I have discussed elsewhere the notion of a relational continuum that may be aligned with the human spiritual journey where the end point is Ultimate Unity – see de Souza (2012).
3. Wilber (1999) describes Unity Consciousness as the point where a person's identity is with the All, with absolutely everything.
4. Sri Aurobindo Ghosh identified five levels of consciousness above the mental, namely, The Higher Mind, the Illumined Mind, Intuition, Overmind and Supermind.
5. Italics in the original quote.
6. Citing some research from ComScore, Carpenter (2009) indicated that MySpace.com attracted more than 114 million visitors in 2007, a 72% increase from the year before, and Facebook attracted 52.2 million visitors, a 270% increase (192).
7. The title of S. Turkle's book is Alone together: Why we expect more from technology and less from each other. Published by Basic Books, New York (2011).

References

Baron-Cohen, S. 2011. *Zero Degrees of Empathy: A New Theory of Human Cruelty*. London: Allen Lane.

Bucke, R. M. 1905. *Cosmic Consciousness: A Study in the Evolution of the Human Mind*. Philadelphia, PA: Innes & Sons.

Carpenter, D. 2009. *The Everything Parent's Guide to Dealing with Bullies*. Avon, MA: F&W Media.

Dossey, L. 2010. "Mind and Neurons: Consciousness and Brain in the Twenty-First Century." In *A New Renaissance: Transforming Science, Spirit and Society*, edited by D. Lorrimer and O. Robinson, 105–119. Edinburgh: Floris Books.

Glatzer, N. N. ed. 1966. *Martin Buber. The Way of Response: Selections from His Writings*. New York: Schocken Books.

Hay, D., and R. Nye. 2006. *The Spirit of the Child. Rev. ed*. London/Philadelphia: Jessica Kingsley.

Hess, M. 2012. "Mirror Neurons, the Development of Empathy, and Digital Story Telling." *Religious Education* 107 (4): 401–414.

Iacoboni, M., and (2008/2009). *Mirroring People: The Science of Empathy and How We Connect with Others*. New York: Picador.

Keysers, C. 2011. *The Empathic Brain: How the Discovery of Mirror Neurons Changes Our Understanding of Human Nature*. Lexington, KY: Social Brain Press.

Maitra, S. K. 2000. *The Meeting of the East and the West in Sri Aurobindo's Philosophy*. Pondicherry: Sri Aurobindo's Ashram.

Ramachandran, V. S. 2011. *The Tell-tale Brain: Unlocking the Mystery of Human Nature*. London: William Heinemann.

Rizzolatti, G., and C. Sinigaglia. 2008. *Mirrors in the Brain. How We Share Our Actions and Emotions*. Oxford: Oxford University Press.

Robinson, K. 2013. "Ken Robinson: How to Escape education's Death Valley." *TED Talks*. Accessed June 11. http://www.youtube.com/watch?v=wX78iKhInsc

de Souza, M. 2009. "Promoting Wholeness and Wellbeing in Education: Exploring Aspects of the Spiritual Dimension." In *International Handbook of Education for Spirituality, Care and Wellbeing*, edited by M. de Souza, L. Francis, J. O'Higgins-Norman and D. Scott, 677–692. Dordrecht: Springer Academic.

de Souza, M. 2012. "Connectedness and Connectedness. The Dark Side of Spirituality: Implications for Education." *International Journal of Children's Spirituality* 17 (4): 291–303.

Turkle, S. 2011. *Alone Together: Why We Expect More from Technology and Less from Each Other*. New York: Basic Books.

Wilber, K. 1999. *The Collected Works of Ken Wilber*. vol. 1. Boston, MA: Shambala.

Let's play at the park! Family pathways promoting spiritual resources to inspire nature, pretend play, storytelling, intergenerational play and celebrations

Kathleen I. Harris

ABSTRACT
Contemporary interest from scholars examining spirituality have suggested that young children have an innately rich spiritual dimension that can be nurtured when they are given opportunities to express it or when such expressions are recognised. Based on direct observations in natural settings, this article addresses the importance of children's spirituality and how outdoor play spaces, especially community parks, can contribute to a child's spiritual development through enriching activities in nature, pretend play, storytelling and intergenerational play. The article also aims to encourage consideration of a variety of strategies that can be used to support the holistic development of a young child and nurture children's spirituality. Supporting a child's spiritual development with playful activities in outdoor spaces can help to identify the child's interests, strengths and creativity through relationships that shape bonds with both families and community.

Rays of sunshine were shining brightly on the playground and lake as three young children enjoyed their time at a neighbourhood community park. Gathered around the sides of a sandbox, the children scooped, poured and shovelled sand into piles and containers. One little girl was moulding the damp sand, experimenting with different shapes. The other two were busy making sand castles and sand cakes for an upcoming party. As one mother stood close to the edge of the sandbox, her daughter looked up with a big grin, saying, 'Mommy, look at the sand cake I am making with my new friend'!

Across from the sandbox, two preschool girls were playing on the swings, with their fathers pushing them. The children could sense their movements as they used their feet to stretch for more speed and soar higher. As they did so, both girls looked up and laughed together at the white, puffy clouds that resembled big marshmallows and cotton candy. Meanwhile, beside the lake, a grandfather and young child observed the shades of orange, yellow, pink and purple in a sunset.

At that exact moment, all six young children described here were capturing the simplicity of spirituality through the joy of outdoor pretend play and by seizing the awe and wonder of the rich outdoor environment offered in their local park. This article is for early childhood teachers and parenting educators and seeks to highlight the importance of outdoor spaces especially community parks, and how they can contribute to a child's holistic development through activities in nature, outdoor pretend play, storytelling, intergenerational play and rituals. It also encourages consideration of a variety of strategies that can be used to nurture the spirituality of young children with imagination, creativity and relationships.

The importance of children's spirituality

Just as each child has unique strengths, personality traits and temperaments, the meaning of spirituality for each child is also distinctive. Spirituality is connected to all human experiences, but it has a particularly close association with the imagination, human creativity and relationships (King, 2008). As adults, we are reminded of a child's natural curiosity and descriptive imagination when we see young children heartfully engaged and playing with their peers. It has been suggested that young children are innately spiritual, and that their rich spiritual dimension can be nurtured when they are given opportunities to express it or when such expressions are positively recognised. Research indicates that from birth, spiritual development occurs in association with other domains of a child's whole development (Miller 2015).

How can early care practitioners and families nurture and honour children's spiritual development? As an early childhood educator, I believe that children's spirituality is intentional and alive with meaningful connections that embrace the holistic development of a young child with joy, zeal and creativity. A child's spirituality is strengthened by making a variety of connections with family members and one's particular community on a regular basis. A child's community could be defined in a variety of ways as a classroom setting, a recreation activity or sports team. When young children share meaningful experiences with families and community, spiritual awareness and attentiveness can become visible.

One way to nurture spiritual awareness and attentiveness for young children is through the notion of space, or the type of environments that nurture spirituality (Hyde 2008). The purposeful use of space with young children can have a lasting effect on learning when they feel comfortable and safe in an environment that will meet their needs. One such nurturing space can be found at a community park, an enriching outdoor space that offers opportunities to experience nature, relationships, fantasy play, wonder and celebrations with families.

Outdoor spaces as contributors to spiritual enrichment

Early childhood teachers and families are increasingly recognising the potential of time outdoors as an opportunity to promote children's development (Pica 2011). The use of outdoor play spaces plays a compelling part of a child's development, as well as connection to the natural world (Nah and Waller 2015). For example, the freedom of having extra space to move freely in the outdoors and experience gross motor activities can develop balance, coordination and spatial awareness for young children. Children love outdoor places where they can run, play tag or roll down grassy hills over and over again. Children use energy while playing outdoors to bring joy and happiness. Sensitivity to nature is essential to our physical and spiritual survival (Louv 2012). For this reason, young children should be given opportunities to dig in the earth, make mud pies, build castles in the sand and take new risks by sliding down a slide or balancing on a seesaw with a friend.

As a teacher of preschool children, I respected and encouraged children's experiences in outdoor natural spaces by including daily sensory walks throughout the neighbourhood near our school, field trips with family members to parks and nature arboretums in each season to experience the life cycles of nature, and a variety of activities at community parks to celebrate classroom rituals to start and end the school year. The variety of learning experiences for children and families, along with how the space is used, is the substance that holds effective outdoor learning programmes together. The connections and ways in which family members and children interact with each other are imperative for outdoor learning (Waite 2011). For this reason, the role of the adult is a major factor component. During outdoor time, early childhood educators and parenting educators can support families to interact informally with children; offering guidance and suggestions that may extend play (Pica 2011). This openness to pedagogy of listening creates opportunities for the child and family to construct ideas and knowledge. When this happens, acceptance to nature can occur; spiritual awareness is receptive by making learning conscious and intentional for the child. This richness makes learning meaningful. New adventures have the potential to nurture a child's spiritual development. Curiosity regarding the unknown can inspire and motivate, moving children towards learning, growth and transcendence (Baumgartner and Buchanan 2010). Therefore, children's spirituality is important and should be nurtured by caring adults, so that children can grow into holistic citizens who are developing not only cognitively, but also socially, emotionally and spirituality (Hyde 2008).

Family components of spirituality: belonging, respect and appreciation

Researchers address three common components of spirituality that cross cultural boundaries: a sense of belonging (Eaude 2003), respect for self and others (Lake, 2004), and an awareness and appreciation of the unknown (Blain and Eady 2002). These components are quietly embedded as children and families play and celebrate together in outdoor natural spaces. For example, when children share, turn take and help one another, and cooperate as a community, they quickly learn that they belong and contribute to society. Family members can guide children's development of belonging when they foster opportunities to promote turn taking and helping, reassuring children they will get a turn, and promote reflections on behaviour (Acar and Torquati 2015). When family members take the time to appreciate outdoor natural spaces, they spark new interests in nature with their child while learning and having fun. Watching butterflies that once started as caterpillars and noticing life cycles of one thing ending and another beginning demonstrates to the young child how things change in nature. Exposing family members to new and interesting facts in nature can be a common thread that brings them together (Satterlee and Cormons 2011). Parenting educators who encourage family members to respect the child's innate spiritual ability to examine and wonder about the natural world foster a child's spiritual development as well as exhibiting respect for oneself and others (Baumgartner and Buchanan 2010). Family members who enrich children's outdoor spiritual experiences offer them new opportunities to express themselves creatively, stretch their imagination, and be continually challenged (Pica 2011).

Opportunities for spiritual awareness in nature

Children love a diverse experience of nature (Oppenheimer 2006). Nature offers young children opportunities to awaken their spiritual curiosity making connections that embrace the holistic development of a young child with joy encouraging zeal and passion. For example, fine motor skills can be developed by picking up red and gold leaves that gently fallen off branches near winter or small pebbles on the path leading to a rock garden and examining the textures on a nature walk; and emotional development is enhanced when a young child sees a butterfly or firefly at night for the first time in late spring, a fawn running through an opening in the park, a rainbow from a waterfall or ducklings with a mother duck under a marsh. Additionally, young children can develop empathy for peers, pets and other living things by carefully observing insects and small frogs on nature walks, walking a pet dog or by playing with peers and taking turns while flying a kite or playing soccer. Young children develop independence and have the ability to sustain relationships when playing cooperatively with peers. Exploration in nature allows children to develop many skills important for later learning and academic success (Gerdes and Miller 2011).

Enriching bonds and authentic relationships can be established between children and adults when they share experiences with nature (Rosenow 2011). For example, during a nature walk, a young child may become curious about an insect found under a rock. The child may ask, 'What's that'? The parent can respond, 'What do you think it is? Let's explore together'. Families are motivational in guiding a child's connection to the natural world (Campbell and Thompson 2013). Young children often have a fascination with the nature and life cycles including birth and growth. To get a child focused on concentrating more in a natural setting, one can ask open-ended questions that engage the various senses. For example, as young children observe and take in the wonders of the outdoor world, language and vocabulary emerge as a key communication to share ideas, dreams, feelings, thoughts and questions about the world around them (Gerdes and Miller 2011).

Nature also offers opportunities for sensory experiences including wind effects, fragrance and texture effects, and seasonal interest in fall colours, winter flowers and berries, spring buds, and summer shadows and shade quality. 'Children must encounter the wild elements with all of their senses: listening, looking, smelling, touching, imagining, even tasking' (Campbell and Thompson, 122). Spiritual activities with nature may include a special place at the park to measure rainfall or snowfall; looking for wildflowers and insects while playing identification games; discussing different types of birds while watching a red squirrel hide acorns for winter or playing with shadows. Materials for observing, documenting, asking questions, and reflecting could include butterfly nets, binoculars and magnifying glasses, to extend spiritual visualisation and an area to enjoy an outdoor picnic for meals and snacks. When we are in touch with natural life, we are in touch with our own soul; the natural world is one of our most reliable windows into wonder, a source of spiritual intelligence (Louv 2012). As a young child continues to care for nature by experiencing nature activities that support the pathways of a child's spiritual development, and also inform the child that the natural world is not separate but a part of who we are in the world, the child will then have the possibility to grow and honour his or her connection to the earth and also humanity (Campbell and Thompson 2013).

Nature can also inspire a sense of fun in young children. For example, when walking on nature trails in parks, families can take a nature walk to share colours, shapes, and textures.

During this activity, it's important for families to allow their child to explore all the natural characteristics of flowers, stems, leaves and petals. While walking near a small lake at a park, a child could also spot a duck and begin to walk like a duck or play peek-a-boo after seeing a turtle go into the shell. A young child may pretend to be a detective looking for different colours of wildflowers or sizes of rocks to solve a mystery. In addition, family members should be receptive to listening and be aware. Near a lake at a park setting, a family member could spot a blue heron and say, 'Look, it's a blue heron looking at us and saying hello on our walk'. While spotting a baby rabbit, a family member can remark that the child was once that tiny and needed a family to take care of the child. Since young children have an innate appreciation of beauty (Daleo 1996), it is important to first look, observe and then begin conversations. At times, it is also permissible for the family member to say, 'I don't know. Let's find out together', while exploring nature at parks. Take time during your visit to the park together to be sensitive to the child's observations, form new investigations, and search for new answers together.

Family members should maintain a spirit of joy as they explore nature in outdoor spaces with young children. For example, while watching a sunset just before an outdoor concert at a park or nature walk, families can observe and discuss how the clouds change brilliant colours and then fade, the first nighttime stars, and how long it takes the sun to fall below the horizon before the moon slowly appears from behind the clouds. As the child observes new discoveries, such as a hummingbird or a monarch butterfly, or watching a spider spin a web, nature can create a spark of awe, wonder and playful spontaneity by giving pleasure and joy to all young children.

Outdoor pretend play at parks and spiritual development

For young children, play is as natural as breathing (Chenfeld 1993). Outdoor play serves as a foundation for supporting leadership and decision-making in early childhood (Sluss 2005). For example, while children are playing with peers at the park, children takes on new roles during fantasy play or find the perfect spot for playing ball, blowing bubbles or jumping rope. Young children have an incredible capacity to use their imagination and creativity to invent new solutions, solve problems and face new challenges by turning them into play. As young children play, they are developing their imagination and their confidence to dream (Mooney 2014). Dreaming is a way for children to use their imagination to create things that have never been created before. In view of the importance that play offers for the development of the whole child, including spiritual development, supportive environments with toys and materials that promote creativity and imagination are very important for all young children.

Parks can provide support for outdoor pretend play. Children go to a park to make sense of the world, most often with peers and by engaging in pretend play (Perry 2001). This can be especially important for young children who are living in urban and/or city environments; outdoor spaces, such as parks, can provide children with explorations, communications and new adventures with peers (Escamilla 2013). In many cases, curiosity emerges through hands-on experiences in nature in which play and discovery are highlighted. For example, outdoor play offers children natural materials. Sand play offers several therapeutic benefits for young children, including developing the sense of touch as they work with the sand's soft texture. Sand play feels good to the hands and feet, is easy to build with, and a creative way for learning about the quality of water (Kenny 2013). Sand play also strengthens arm, wrist and hand muscles through grasping, shovelling and scooping motions. Sandboxes offer children opportunities for creativity, pretend play and socialisation with peers, as well as relieving stress (McNulty 2007). In addition, young children can create pretend play with other natural materials found in parks, such as tree branches, leaves, rocks, sand, acorns and water. In addition, large spaces can allow children to use their whole body to investigate and carry out plans for play without restrictions on loud noise or activity (Perry 2003). For example, many parks provide play objects in the shape of fire engines, rocket ships, cars, tractors, and other objects that can stimulate pretend play (Scarlett et al. 2005). On many occasions during outdoor pretend play, children may follow a process and sequence of steps that encourage and promote spiritual awareness and participation. The four steps towards spiritual development in outdoor pretend play include commencement, collaboration, construction and community.

Commencement

During this first step of outdoor pretend play, children decide whom they wish to play with and invite peers into a play scenario. Often, when young children play at parks with peers, new friendships can easily develop. As young children play alongside each other, they become interested not only in their own play, but also in what others do (Scarlett et al. 2005). This shared interest in each other's nature play can lead to the building of friendships as children go on a scavenger hunt or look for animals together. If there is mutual interest with toys and materials, such as swings or a sandbox in the park environment, children may be more eager to share their passions and time together by initiating play commencement conversations.

Families can encourage children during the commencement phase of pretend play by coaching and prompting their child to use friendly phrases with peers: 'I see a boy around your age by the sandbox all alone without a friend. Let's go up to him and say hello. You could ask him if he would like to play trucks with you in the sandbox'. Alternatively, a family member can set up toys or materials on a picnic table, blanket, playground or sandbox to encourage children to engage in conversations and playful interaction with one another. For example, setting buckets and shovels in the sandbox or placing bubbles and a ball on a blanket can suggest opportunities for motivating pretend play. Once children make eye contact with the toys or materials, the commencement of pretend play can proceed spontaneously and intentionally.

Collaboration

The second step of outdoor pretend play gives children time to collaborate with one another, feel comfortable being with each other and negotiate together the themes and specific play roles for each child. During this step, children take time to listen and work together on a play plan. Often, however, while conceptualising a plan for pretend play, children may have trouble with directions and become stuck cognitively on how to determine certain play roles. Depending on the children's ages and abilities, family members may support them during this stage by conceptualising and considering creative roles for pretend play or suggesting imaginative 'what if' play scenarios that are developmentally appropriate and related to the children's interests.

Construction

In this third step of outdoor pretend play, children are motivated and engaged to participate. They may use words to create additional play scenarios (e.g., 'Let's make birthday cakes and also cupcakes with sprinkles for Billy's party'. They may also use words to describe imaginary objects and actions (e.g., 'I'm building a fort'). During this step, children are constructing and acting out their fantasy roles and developing current and new themes. Children enjoy each other's company during pretend play by experimenting, organising, discovering new ideas, expressing their feelings, achieving new goals, taking turns, and sharing and socialising together. During outdoor pretend play, children may offer and take suggestions from other peers (e.g., in the sandbox, 'That's a great idea! Let's make a post office next to the fire station'! or while on the swings, 'After this, let's go on the slide and teeter-totter together'). As they construct pretend play, children are characters in their own stories and enjoy the spirit of play. They use their language and nonverbal skills to shape and maintain play by incorporating others' ideas and suggestions.

Community

The final step towards establishing spiritual outdoor pretend play, and perhaps the most important one, is community. Children who are socially accepted into a community have experienced the beginning stages of positive social skills (for example, greeting peers, turn taking, helping peers, following directions, early stages of empathy and manners) and friendships with peers. As a result, they are accustomed to showing kindness to others, have a good start towards understanding and following rules, and recognise other people's feelings (Odom 2002). During play, children respect each other and participate fully with peers. When children come together during play to know one another and discover what each child has in common, they celebrate the humanity and uniqueness of individuals. Community involves connecting, belonging and sharing interests and dreams with one another. It also includes discovering who your neighbours are within the community. For the esteemed children's television personality Fred Rogers, neighbours and community were sacred, valued and appreciated 'Seeing the eternal in your neighbour, that divine presence that allows us to show mercy to our neighbour –and to receive it' (Hollingsworth 2005, 79). Appreciating and honouring our neighbours and community encourages the dispositions of compassion and kindness. These dispositions can create an atmosphere in outdoor spaces of caring attachments for storytelling, play across developmental life cycles and enriching family rituals and ceremonies to celebrate milestones.

Storytelling at the park with children

How often has a child said to you, 'Tell me a story'? Stories not only entertain but also interweave our history, our aspirations and the values of our culture (Dermond 2007). Stories are what we remember. 'They are the heart of a people and pathways of the soul' (Daleo 1996, 90). A child's play, whether constructive or dramatic, is in effect practice in storytelling, as the child creates or recreates plot, motive, character and setting (Jones 2011). One of the best ways to share oral storytelling is with a family member, especially a grandparent or elder with whom the child is comfortable and enjoys spending time.

Oral storytelling gives children opportunities to stimulate their imagination and communication skills, and it enhances their social literacy by building community in a unique way that is different from reading stories in picture books (Berkowitz 2011). Just like nature, stories are a springboard to compassion and spiritual awareness because they can stimulate feelings and open the heart. Spontaneous storytelling allows children to be themselves, share feelings openly and think creatively without few burdens or obligations. When children are given freedom to share story ideas with family members and/or peers, a magical capacity may emerge incorporating fantasy and humour. Experiential learning can take place when young children are given opportunities during pretend play to create their own stories (Kenny 2013). Stories are representations of our day-to-day experiences, whether caught in standard prose, musical lyrics, images, dance or drama (Jones 2011). At a park setting, oral storytelling can take place while the participants are sitting on a park bench, moving gently on a swing, enjoying a picnic or making sand castles. Children's ideas from oral storytelling can take their imaginations to new levels, heightening their engagement by supporting learning through the invitation to role-playing and performance (Berkowitz 2011). Dramatising stories gives children opportunities to actively choose and make sense of characters, settings and events. As a result, children gain a sense of control over themselves and their situation (Paley 2004). As children take turns communicating with peers and family members during oral storytelling, they begin to appreciate different points of view and work together to resolve conflicts (Berkowitz 2011).

Oral storytelling can be initiated by family members or by the child. Relaxed playtimes in a park setting offer excellent opportunities to tell stories. Uplifting stories from family members can be very popular because children are greatly influenced by role models. Stories that contain repetitive verses, such as *Brown Bear, Brown Bear, What Do You See* (Martin, 1996) or *We're Going on a Bear Hunt* (Rosen, 1989), give children opportunities to participate and extend the story. While telling a story, family members should consider asking open-ended questions about the characters and parts of the story to encourage dialogue and imagination. Oral storytelling offers young children an avenue to listen, participate and learn while playing. Families can also document these experiences by taping the child's voice on an iPad or tablet and taking digital pictures. Learning experiences that can awaken a higher level of engagement and deeper curiosity in a child and that motivate the child to continue investigating and learning have great educational value (Dewey 1938).

Intergenerational Synergy: play across the circle of life at the park

Research indicates the importance of intergenerational experiences for children's spiritual development (Powell 2009; Roberto, 2012). Extended family members such as grandparents, who may often participate in caring for the children, are an important source of support for families (Berger and Riojas-Cortez 2012). Many grandparents enjoy special times with their grandchildren at the park. Elder play with young children offers time for contemplation and solitude (Jones 2011). Contemplation may include watching birds, taking quiet nature walks with an awareness of plants, clouds, trees, and sunsets, or fishing together. Grandparents also enjoy sharing precious memories with grandchildren by reminiscing about their own childhood and the games they played when they were little. During this special time together, a young child comes to know the grandparent as an individual and discovers similarities between them as well as differences. When we begin to give children an appreciation of the past, not just through scattered facts, but as a thread in the tapestry of our lives, then the richness of past experience can be appreciated and respected (Daleo 1996). As stories are shared together, history takes on meaning and children gain access to that shared experience. The past becomes a bridge to the present and future (Daleo 1996).

In some situations, just taking time to sit quietly in silence can be very soothing and calming for a young child. By doing this, a child can be responsive to the natural rhythm and energy of the universe. It takes energy and effort to support a child in developing the quietness and peace amidst which inner calmness and spiritual self-awareness can develop (Dermond 2007). In many cases, quiet times enhance the development of intrapersonal intelligence, which Howard Gardner (1997) refers to as having an understanding of yourself, or knowing who you are, what you can do, what you want to do and how you react to things. In moments of solitude, new ideas can be created, problems are solved, and an understanding of inspiration and motivation in young children can grow.

Promoting mastery motivation during outdoor play at the park

During the early years, play impacts a child's motivation (Bodrova and Leong 2011). Harter (1975, 370) described motivation as, 'a necessary internal criterion to undergird success, curiosity, a preference for challenge, and working for one's own satisfaction.' At a park setting, family members, siblings and peers are all potential partners in children's motivation (Hauser-Cram 1998). Play activities at the park such as riding a bike, roller skating or playing ball offer children multiple opportunities to practice mastery motivation by providing tasks in which the goal is learning (i.e., developing different strategies) rather than performance (i.e., focusing on correct or incorrect responses) (Stipek 1996).

> Mastery motivation is described as a force that stimulates an individual to attempt independently, in a focused manner, to solve a problem or master a task which is at least challenging for the child. (Morgan, Harmon, and Maslin-Cole 1990, 318)

In an outdoor setting, young children respond to the environment in a very unself-conscious and natural way, taking the opportunity to explore with their senses and live in the rhythms of their bodies. Providing opportunities for mastery motivation and self-confidence to a child supports all domains of development, including the spiritual domain, by learning though doing.

Because motivation is often intrinsic for young children, it is important for family members to provide them with activities at a community park that offer opportunities to learn, not just to be correct or incorrect. For example, various games with peers at the park can explore ways to solve a problem. On other occasions, while the child is working actively at accomplishing the task, it's very important for family members to support the child's activities in ways that will not interfere with autonomy. For example, if a child becomes frustrated climbing a jungle gym or gets tired on a nature walk or while flying a kite, the family member can offer support, positive praise, encouragement and suggestions rather than direct commands. In this way, young children have the chance to be spiritual explorers through being actively engaged in a search for meanings about the world around them.

Spiritual wonder and awe: celebrating cycles of nature

Wonder is the foundation for spirituality (Wolf 1996). Children's wonder is nurtured when young children are given time to observe and meditate on the beauty of nature. All children are born with curiosity and a desire to learn about the world (Hauser-Cram 1998). The capacity to wonder is one of the most critically important things that we carry forth from our childhood into adulthood (Brown 2012). Wonder is also the playful part of learning that sustains potential for the future (Meir, Engel, and Taylor 2010). For example, sharing the different cycles of nature with young children on an 'I Spy' discovery walk through a park to explore connections between living things can create moments to appreciate beauty. Allowing children to whisper their dreams to tree fairies during a nature walk, examine colours on rocks, compare two shapes of leaves during autumn, gaze up at the clouds to daydream and be surprised at the height and grace of a blue heron flying over a lake at sunset support their inborn sense of wonder. Wonder can take us beyond a purely earthly outlook on life by enticing us to entertain new possibilities with joy and hope; it also encourages an open-ended approach to life (Fuller 2006).

Young children have an incredible capacity for wonder, awe, and mystery (Mooney 2014). While playing with peers and walking with family members in parks, young children observe small things as well as large ones: tiny insects on the ground, spider webs and daddy long legs in a corner of a sandbox, rocks and stones on a nature walk, tadpoles and frogs in a creek, shadows of tree branches, clouds dancing across the sky, and the shimmering rays of light through summer leaves. Children often display drama, surprise and joy as they are awakened to the mysteries of nature and the known and unknown. Wonder is a core foundation of children's spirituality (Fuller 2006). For example, when families give children opportunities to enjoy moments of curiosity and wonder outdoors, time can slip away along with the hurry of a busy life as the child is surrounded by enchantment with the present. As children become aware of the beauty and wonder of outdoor spaces, they may become curious and eager to investigate, examine and learn more about it. Wonder offers all of us an invitation to go beyond self-centred perspectives of the world and connects to our affective capacity for empathy and care (Fuller 2006). Two simple words, 'I wonder', describe one of the most defining characteristics of childhood (Meir, Engel, and Taylor 2010).

Family celebrations at the park

Celebrations with families can range from a simple rhythm of meals and family gatherings to wider festivities involving communities (Daleo 1996). Celebrations give families a sense of themselves and also opportunities to enjoy stories, songs, games and laughter together. Sharing quality time together at a park is one way in which families can establish rituals and ceremonies that are unique to their values and traditions. Child psychologists indicate the importance of establishing rituals early in a child's life (Florian 2001). For example, rituals at bedtime close for the day with a sense of comfort; rituals at dinner demonstrate family roles and are considered important sources of security. Rituals incorporate the child into the family, giving him or her role, a set of expectations and an identity (Florian 2001). One way for families to celebrate rituals and ceremonies at parks is by celebrating the seasonal solstice together.

Across all cultures, families come together in observance of the progression of time, in recognition of our relationship to earth (Oppenheimer 2006). When families spend time together to celebrate reunions and birthday milestones, especially at outdoor spaces such as parks, they can look back over the past year, remembering where they were, what they did and who was present in their lives. During this time, they can also anticipate the future, considering how the family dynamics may change in the coming year (Oppenheimer 2006). Family celebrations typically include several important elements. First, all family members should have a contributing role. To make the celebration come alive, there should be traditional activities. For example, during an autumn festival, families may celebrate the apple harvest or bring pumpkins to the park to celebrate a fall harvest. Or they can make applesauce or pumpkin pudding, or take nature walks and create nature wreaths of pine cones, acorns and autumn leaves. The celebration could conclude with stories of cutting an apple in half and finding the star, autumn songs, arts and crafts, and dances to celebrate the harvest. Family celebrations, rituals, concerts and ceremonies at the park thus become a precious memory that will live inside the hearts of young children.

Conclusion

Young children's natural spiritual qualities are similar across cultures, socio-economic groups, communities and families (Miller 2015). Authentic and imaginative spiritual play at parks and various inspiring nature activities invites and supports us to wholeness, opens us to our souls and hearts, and motivates us to live. When we bring playfulness to our relationships, desires and dreams, we open ourselves deeply to family and community connections making them more meaningful and soul-nourishing (Mooney 2014). Awakening a child's spiritual development with playful activities in outdoor environments can help to identify the child's passions, strengths, motivation and creativity. Bonds with families and communities are shaped through relationships, stories, outdoor pretend play and celebrations. Miller's (2015) research regarding children's spirituality describes five spiritual resources with which every child is born: (a) a natural love of spiritual rituals and ceremonies, (b) a capacity for spiritual awareness and intuitive guidance, care, and empathy, (c) a desire to be helpful, contributing, and sharing, (d) an innate sense of the oneness of family, and (e) a connection with nature and curiosity regarding the passage of human growth and life cycles. Offering opportunities for children to play, learn and embrace nature at community parks can promote and support these five spiritual resources by contributing synergy and wonder to a young child's spiritual development.

The child's spiritual development is most righteous of our attention and support as family members and community (Miller 2015). An appropriate outdoor space such as a community park, can serve effectively as a natural and spiritual setting for all young children. Many early childhood and parenting educators are now recognising and advocating to families the importance of outdoor play for children. They are recognising that if the appropriate outdoor space is available to foster a sense of creativity and outdoor play, the whole child may progress in all domains of learning and development (Rosenow 2011). The community park is a place where young children can play, breathe, examine, question and celebrate the world of rhythms inside their hearts and souls.

> Each of us needs to withdraw from the cares which will not withdraw from us. We need hours of aimless wandering or spates of time sitting on park benches, observing the mysterious world of ants and the canopy of treetops. (Angelou 1994, 139)

Disclosure statement

No potential conflict of interest was reported by the author.

References

Acar, I., and J. Torquati. 2015. "The Power of Nature: Developing Prosocial Behavior toward Nature and Peers through Nature-based Activities." *Young Children* 70 (5): 62–71.

Angelou, M. 1994. *Wouldn't Take Nothing for My Journey Now*. New York: Bantam.

Baumgartner, J. J., and T. Buchanan. 2010. "Supporting Each Child's Spirit." *Young Children* 65 (2): 90–94.

Berger, E. H., and M. Riojas-Cortez. 2012. *Parents as Partners in Education: Families and Schools Working Together*. Upper Saddle River, NJ: Pearson.

Berkowitz, D. 2011. "Oral Storytelling: Building Community through Dialogue, Engagement, and Problem Solving." *Young Children* 66 (2): 36–40.

Blain, M., and S. Eady. 2002. "The WOW Factor: Spiritual Development through Science." *International Journal of Children's Spirituality* 25 (2): 125–135.

Bodrova, E., and D. J. Leong. 2011. "Revisiting Vygotskian Perspectives on Play and Pedagogy." In *Rethinking Play and Pedagogy in Early Childhood Education*, edited by S. Rogers, 60–72. New York: Routledge.

Brown, W. P. 2012. "Wisdom and Child's Play: Proverbs and Paideia." In *Understanding Children's Spirituality: Theology, Research, and Practice*, edited by K. E. Lawson, 26–38. Eugene, OR: Cascade Books.

Campbell, D., and S. Thompson. 2013. "Naturally Speaking – Parents, Children, Teachers in Dialogue with Nature." In *Nature Education with Young Children*, edited by D. R. Meier and S. Sisk-Hilton, 105–122. New York: Routledge.

Chenfeld, M. B. 1993. *Teaching in the Key of Life*. Washington, DC: National Association for the Education of Young Children.

Daleo, M. S. 1996. *Curriculum of Love: Cultivating the Spiritual Nature of Children*. Charlottesville, VA: Grace Publishing and Communications.

Dermond, S. U. 2007. *Calm and Compassionate Children: A Handbook*. New York: Celestial Arts.

Dewey, J. 1938. *Experience and Education*. New York: MacMillan.

Eaude, T. 2003. "Shining Lights in Unexpected Corners: New Angles on Young Children's Spiritual Development." *International Journal of Children's Spirituality* 8 (2): 151–162.

Escamilla, I. M. 2013. "Drawing, Photographs, and Painting – Learning about the Natural World in an Urban Preschool." In *Nature Education with Young Children*, edited by D. R. Meier and S. Sisk-Hilton, 194–215. New York: Routledge.

Florian, A. 2001. *Creating and Celebrating Classroom Rituals: Sign, Symbol, Word and Song*. Notre Dame, IN: Ave Maria Press.

Fuller, R. C. 2006. *Wonder*. Charlotte, NC: University of North Carolina Press.

Gardner, H. 1997. *Multiple Intelligences: New Horizons*. New York: Basic Books.

Gerdes, J., and J. L. Miller. 2011. "Experiences in Nature: A Pathway to Standards." In *Spotlight on young children and nature*, edited by A. Shillady, 24–30. Washington, DC: National Association for the Education of Young Children.

Harter, S. 1975. "Developmental Differences in the Manifestation of Mastery Motivation on Problem-solving Tasks." *Child Development* 46: 370–378.

Hauser-Cram, P. 1998. "I Think I Can, I Think I Can: Understanding and Encouraging Mastery Motivation in Young Children." *Young Children* 52 (4): 67–71.

Hollingsworth, A. 2005. *The Simple Faith of Mister Rogers: Spiritual Insights from the World's Most Beloved Neighbor*. Lexington, KY: Thomas Nelson.

Hyde, B. 2008. *Children and Spirituality: Searching for Meaning and Connectedness*. Philadelphia, PA: Jessica Kingsley Publishers.

Jones, E. 2011. "Play across the Life Cycle: From Initiative to Integrity to Transcendence." *Young Children* 66 (4): 84–90.

Kenny, E. K. 2013. *Forest Kindergartens: The Cedarsong Way*. Vashon, WA: Cedarsong Nature School.

King, U. 2008. *The Search for Spirituality: Our Global Quest for a Spiritual Life*. New York: Blue Ridge.

Lake, V. 2004. "Ante up: Reconsidering Classroom Management Philosophies so Every Child is a Winner." *Early Child Development and Care* 174 (6): 565–574.

Louv, R. 2012. *The Nature Principle: Reconnecting with Life in a Virtual Age*. Chapel Hill, NC: Algonquin Books.

Martin, B. 1996. *Brown Bear, Brown Bear, What Do You See?*. New York: Henry Holt.

McNulty, W. 2007. "Superheroes and Sand Play: Using the Archetype through the Healing Journey." In *Using Superheroes in Counseling and Play Therapy*, edited by L. C. Rubin, 69–81. New York: Springer.

Meir, D., B. S. Engel, and B. Taylor. 2010. *Playing for Keeps: Life and Learning on a Public School Playground*. New York: Teachers College Press.

Miller, L. 2015. *The Spiritual Child: The New Science on Parenting for Health and Lifelong Thriving*. New York: St. Martin's Press.

Mooney, T. J. 2014. *Like a Child: Restoring the Awe, Wonder, Joy, and Resilience of the Human Spirit*. Woodstock, VT: Christian Journeys.

Morgan, G. A., R. J. Harmon, and C. A. Maslin-Cole. 1990. "Mastery Motivation: Definition and Measurement." *Early Education and Development* 1: 318–339.

Nah, K. O., and T. Waller. 2015. "Outdoor Play in Preschools in England and South Korea: Learning from Polyvocal Methods." *Early Child Development and Care* 185 (11–12): 2010–2025.

Odom, S. L. 2002. *Widening the Circle: Including Children with Disabilities in Preschool Programs*. New York: Teachers College Press.

Oppenheimer, S. 2006. *Heaven on Earth: A Handbook for Parents of Young Children*. Great Barrington, MA: Steiner Books.

Paley, V. G. 2004. *A Child's Work*. Chicago, IL: University of Chicago Press.

Perry, J. P. 2001. *Outdoor Play: Teaching Strategies with Young Children*. New York: Teachers College Press.

Perry, J. P. 2003. "Making Sense of Outdoor Pretend Play." *Young Children* 58 (4): 26–30.

Pica, R. 2011. "Taking Movement Education Outdoors." *Young Children* 66 (4): 58–60.

Powell, K. 2009. "Is the Era of Age Segregation over? An Interview with Kara Powell" *Leadership* 30 (3): 43–48.

Roberto, J. 2012. "Our Future is Intergenerational." *Christian Education Journal* 9 (1): 105–120.

Rosen, M. 1989. *We're Going on a Bear Hunt*. New York: Margaret K. McEldberry.

Rosenow, N. 2011. "Learning to Love the Earth … and Each Other." In *Spotlight on Young Children and Nature*, edited by A. Shillady, 4–7. Washington, DC: National Association for the Education of Young Children.

Satterlee, D. J., and G. D. Cormons. 2011. "Sparking Interest in Nature-family Style." In *Spotlight on Young Children and Nature*, edited by A. Shillady, 15–19. Washington, DC: National Association for the Education of Young Children.

Scarlett, W. G., S. Naudeau, D. Salonius-Pasternak, and I. Ponte. 2005. *Children's Play*. Thousand Oaks, CA: Sage.

Sluss, D. J. 2005. *Supporting Play: Birth to Age Eight*. New York: Delmar Learning.

Stipek, D. J. 1996. "Motivation and Instruction." In *Handbook of Educational Psychology*, edited by D. Berlinger and R. Calfee, 85–113. New York: Macmillan.

Waite, S. 2011. *Children Learning outside the Classroom: From Birth to Eleven*. London, England: Sage.

Wolf, A. D. 1996. *Nurturing the Spirit in Non-sectarian Classrooms*. Santa Rosa, CA: Parent Child Press.

Children's spirituality and theologising with children: the role of 'context'

Annemie Dillen

ABSTRACT

Reflections on 'child theology' are often linked to contexts of schools (especially in German literature) or parishes/congregations, where children's spirituality can be nourished or where they can be supported in their theological thinking. This article will broaden these more 'traditional' contexts, and will deal with examples of children's spirituality and theologizing with children in a context of a hospital or after a migration experience. On the basis of examples of research in various international contexts, especially with children who had to deal with complex personal or political related challenges or even trauma (illness, murder, war, migration, ...), a more fundamental question will be asked: what is the role of the context in which children develop their own spirituality and it which others (mostly adults) support them in theologizing? Examples of recent empirical research will be discussed in dialogue with the postcolonial practical theological work of Courtney Goto on the 'idolisation of context' (2018). Theological questions will be asked about the relationship between 'spirituality' and 'theologizing' on the one hand and universal/global/general characteristics or more local, contextual approaches on the other hand.

1. Introduction

Reflections on children's spirituality and on 'theologising with children' are often linked to contexts of schools (especially in German literature) or parishes/congregations, where children's spirituality can be nourished or where they can be supported in their theological thinking. The literature about children's spirituality and theology in families is more limited, most probably because parents are not professionals. Thus, the topic of children's spirituality gets less attention from scholars who also work as trainers/educators for professionals. For this contribution, the term 'context' is broadened beyond traditional 'learning contexts'. One way of broadening could be to study children's spirituality in sport activities, in relation to gaming or during holiday camps. Research in this field is barely existent. However, context does not only refer to concrete situations in which children experience or express their spirituality, it also refers to aspects related to specific religions, to ethnicity and to socio-economic status, and even to gender. This last element is sometimes explicitly studied, e.g. when the spirituality of female adolescent girls was described by Joyce Mercer (2008). Various other aspects of context are only seldomly explicitly thematised.

This article first describes this lack of attention for 'context' and searches for possible explanations. In a second step the theoretical reflection is confronted with the critical, postcolonial analysis of practical theologian Courtney Goto (2018) about the 'idolisation of context'. In a third step I describe recent and ongoing research projects, all conducted at my own university, but in a variety of cultural contexts, and focus specifically on the role of the context. In the conclusion I will develop suggestions for future research and practices.

Before describing the role and the meaning of context in relation to children's spirituality and theologising with children, this article should be situated within the context of the author. I write as a Roman-Catholic practical theologian, working as a professor at a Faculty for Theology and Religious Studies in Flanders (the Northern part of Belgium), in the region where I was born. Additionally, I am chairing the Interdiocesan Council for Family Ministry in the Flemish Church. This article is mainly influenced by my work as a supervisor of various international PhD students and a leader of a specific project about children's spirituality in the Philippines. My experiences as a mother, with my own school-aged children in a middle-class Belgian context, are quite different from the experiences of the children worldwide who participate in the research described in this article. This difference can also partly be attributed to the secularised context in Belgium. This short description might help to situate the research presented below, and especially the possible biases due to this positionality.

2. A lack of attention for 'context'

2.1. What is missing?

The Canadian practical theologian Dave Csinos demonstrates in an article of 2018 how 'cultural aspects' or 'context' are only discussed to a limited extent in most research on children's spirituality and theology. He explains how various authors mention the role of culture, but do not consider it as a relevant factor in the analysis of empirical data, neither in the design of the study. He critically describes this 'cultural oblivion' in relation to the often cited research of David Hay and Rebecca Nye (2006). Csinos argues that although they describe how 'spirituality is culturally mediated and always exists within particular cultural contexts' (2018, 55), they do not really take this into account when they describe the qualitative empirical work of Nye. A rather homogeneous group of children is interviewed by Nye. Their religious background is somewhat diverse, but they generally fit under 'Caucasian', middle class children, living in a town in England. Based on this research, 'relational consciousness' is considered as an important characteristic for children's spirituality. Csinos describes various other pieces of research, where authors are not blind to the role of the cultural context, but still do not pay enough attention to it (see also Csinos 2020). He writes about these studies that 'while, they may open windows into *what* children think – their theological products – many of them overlook *how* children think, that is, the processes by which they generate their beliefs' (60). There are more and more qualitative studies about children's spirituality, but most of them are generally in European, Australian or North-American contexts with middle-class children with a (post-) Christian or secular background. Some studies compare results from various countries and have a cross-cultural design, but even then, Csinos argues, the focus is mostly on what children from these various backgrounds have in common, and less on the diversity or on the production of theology or on the process of developing a form of spirituality in dialogue with cultural, contextual elements and with each other or with a larger community (58).

He considers the work of Joyce Mercer as an exception (2004; Mercer, Matthews, and Walz 2004). She explicitly describes theoretically and empirically how cultural contexts, influenced by capitalist characteristics and especially also issues of class, interact which children's spirituality. Csinos writes about Mercer: 'Not only does she hold that the relationship between a culture and its individual members is mutually influential, but she also assumes that cultures do not necessarily contain internal consensus, for she admits that within congregations, the experience of and meaning ascribed to practices will vary among members, and she states that shared practices are sites of resistance (Mercer, Matthews, and Walz 2004, 250–251). Furthermore, Mercer reveals a complex and fluid understanding of culture in her thoughts surrounding the multiplicity of communities that are operative in the lives of individuals and the competitive nature of cultural influence.' (Csinos 2018, 60).

Csinos also refers to his own research where he describes each congregation in which he was a participant observer, doing ethnographic fieldwork. Three major aspects are important: (1) taking culture into account does not only mean referring to 'products' (as if children's spirituality is something static), but especially also to the process (where mutual interaction with the culture is very important). (2) It is not only an individual process, but also a group process, where children during qualitative empirical interviews construct spirituality and theology together in response to the researcher's questions. (3) And finally, culture matters in every stage of the research design, Csinos argues.

After this critical analysis, I have three major questions, which Csinos only answers partly in his article. First, why are there many studies and authors not paying enough attention to culture? Secondly, is this critique of Csinos on cultural oblivion also applicable to studies that deal with the specific contexts of 'schools' on the one hand and 'congregations' or 'parishes' on the other hand? Thirdly, what could be appropriate alternatives or could this critical review of existing studies be applied to other studies as well?

2.2. How to understand and explain this cultural oblivion?

There are various possible explanations for why the cultural context is not often explicitly studied in research on children's spirituality. A first way to understand this is because of the presumed or hoped for universality of the results. Of course, qualitative empirical researchers know that the context in which their research takes place and the limited scale of this research, does not allow for easy generalisations. However, on a more theoretical level, studies as the one of Hay and Nye seem to suppose that the theoretical conclusions about 'relational awareness' are valuable elsewhere as well (2006). Especially when this goes hand in hand with biological argumentations, as Hay and Nye develop, the need to focus on the particularities of the context seems to disappear.

A second reason why specific attention to cultural contexts is limited, might be found in a general blindness for issues such as class, race and ethnicity within contexts where researchers and the children who are studied often belong to a cultural majority or to a dominant group in society. As we learn from critical race studies and theology that takes whiteness into consideration, those who are in dominant positions often forget to name their own position as 'coloured', just as that of others (Wollrad 2005). The same is true for studies about masculinity, for instance. Decades ago, feminist theologians criticised the absence of specific attention for women's perspectives. It is only very recently that theologians are discovering that masculinity is not automatically the standard or dominant context of experiencing reality and are studying the relationship between ideas and experiences about masculinity and theology (Kummer 2019).

A third reason related to cultural oblivion, can be that 'intersectionality' is not yet a major perspective in the area of children's spirituality. A majority of studies about children's spirituality is developed in North-American, European and Australian contexts. Especially in Europe, the awareness about intersectionality as an important perspective for research is not so widespread. Intersectionality means that persons are considered at the intersection of various axes, not only in gender matters or other binary distinctions. One person is at the same moment also positioned on the axis of socio-economic status (with less or more financial means), on the axis of religion (related to belonging to a majority or to a minority), or the axis of ethnicity or race (related to all kinds of privileges or experiences of powerlessness). The way power is attributed depends on their position on these constructed axes. On some they might experience many privileges, on others not. Age is of course also a similar axis referring to people's social identity. The power attributed to these positions and the position people take is fluid and might change over time. Very often, researchers tend to focus on one axis, in this case the one related to age (child-adult), in order to make things visible and to give a voice to underrepresented groups. The study of children's spirituality and theology has been – at least implicitly – influenced by what can be called 'strategic essentialism' (Spivak, 1988; see also Mercer 2005, 20) researchers know that children are very different, and that one cannot speak about a homogeneous experience as 'a child'. However, for strategic reasons, namely to explain how children's own views are important and to show how they are as valuable as adult perspectives, they pretend as if there is something essential in children or in children's spirituality even. This approach has worked for some time, but it is important to stretch the research on children's spirituality a bit further now and to take issues on 'intersectionality' into account, beyond contextual and cultural blindness.

A fourth possible explanation for the limited attention to culture in studies on children's spirituality and theology, might be found in the similarity to 'contextual theologies' and a critical view on it. Judith Gruber, who self-identifies as an 'intercultural theologian', describes how various ways of doing theology (especially systematic theology) from specific cultural contexts, often succeed in paying attention to a specific context and its value, but struggle with the connection with more universal aspects and may be considered as particular 'niches', without much relevance for broader theological theories (2018). A similar argument is made by Knippe and Kupari (2020) who describe the state of the art of (empirical) research on 'lived religion', in relation to theories within the field of religious studies. Further research has to be done in this regard, but it is worthwhile to investigate whether this is also true for specific studies on children's spirituality with particular minority groups or in under researched areas. It is, anyhow, particularly difficult to link empirical work to broader theoretical and theological work. Empirical and practical theologians claim the value of doing this, but it is nevertheless very often difficult to explain the exact relations between empirical results and theoretical views.

In this article I try to construct a meta-reflection based on empirical studies on children's spirituality in various contexts. However, much more work has to be done in this regard, in order to avoid the possible danger that the study of children's spirituality is both in its empirical and in its theoretical aspect a mainly fragmented body of literature, where 'context' then only functions as a way to continue the research and to claim innovative results each time when similar work is done in a different place.

When Csinos explains that, from his study in very diverse congregations, he learned how children, as a small group, co-construct their spirituality, in dialogue with the researcher, he gives an example of how explicit attention to the context does not only help to discover something about that particular context, but also teaches something about the process of developing spirituality, which might be more theoretical, and again, more 'universal'.

2.3. Relations with traditional 'contexts' such as schools and parishes/ congregations

So far, I presumed that Csinos' remarks about the limited attention to cultural contexts and my own ways to understand and explain this, make sense, especially because we speak about 'cultures', and especially also about aspects related to ethnicity, race or class. But, when classical contexts such as 'schools' and 'parishes' or 'congregations' are studied, at least this particular aspect of the context (institutional learning), is taken seriously. At least theoretically, it is presumed that the teacher and the class, as a group, play an important role for the individual pupil. Children co-construct their spirituality in relationship with the teacher and the other students. But it is certainly a point for further discussion and research to clarify the role of this specific context and to question whether children would express their spirituality in similar ways when they are at home, or in a totally different setting. Very often interviews are happening in a particular context, a class or a preparation for confirmation or first communion, because this is the most convenient setting to reach children.

However, there is research about the relationship between the school and children's spirituality. Didier Pollefeyt, leads a large research project in Australia and Belgium, where he investigates the religious views of children, adolescents and teachers, in order to be able to say something about the catholic identity of the school (2014). Here, it is presumed that the identity of the institution is also influenced by the way in which the children (and the teachers and the parents) think. This research tries to stimulate Catholic identity in a particular way, under the key term 'catholic dialogue school', and thus also hope to enhance the second naiveté way of thinking about religion of children and adolescents. In this research line, the role of the school context is discussed on the basis of a dialogue between theological views and empirical cross-sectional studies of participants in the school life.

Other researchers, such as the German Catholic empirical theologians Ulrich Riegel or Friedrich Schweitzer, are setting up intervention studies in schools, in order to know more about specific outcomes of teaching practices (Riegel and Kindermann 2016; Schweitzer and Boschki 2018). They would focus more on a longitudinal approach or specific intervention study with pre- and post-measures. The complexity of this methodology however, is that some contextual elements are clearly considered in the empirical study (e.g. the role of field trips to a church within religious education in a German school context), but various other contextual elements have to be put between brackets in these studies, which are mainly quantitative, in order to compare pre- and post-results. What is the role of the personality of the teacher, of the global cultural, (post-) secular context, or the middle-class contexts of the students in Germany, etc.?

Much more could be said about Csinos' analysis in relation to schools and parishes/congregations. Here, I will proceed with the critical analysis of another practical theologian, Courtney Goto and then conclude with concrete case studies about children.

3. Idolisation of the context?

The analysis of the lack of specific attention to 'context' by Dave Csinos is probably partly inspired by his self-identification as a practical theologian. Many practical theologians all over the world would state that attention for specific context is particularly relevant. The American theologian Courtney Goto does not question the relevance of context, but the idolisation of it. She writes: 'Unless we question the normativity of how we speak of, research, and teach "context", we create a powerful god. By challenging what it is taken for granted when we discuss "context", we can engage the process of reconstructing ideas and practices with greater awareness' (2018, xv).

Goto explains how many practical theological approaches try to take 'context' seriously, but might do injustice to particular people and congregations. She explains how various theologians do research about particular groups as 'outsiders', from a purely academic perspective. Inside knowledge might get lost in that way. Others train leaders of congregations to act as researchers themselves. They might however expect that the 'local leaders' adopt the methods and approaches of academic practical theology, which does not necessarily fit with their own ways of exploring the context and the way in which people think and practice. She speaks about the harm of *epistemic injustice* in research. 'Training the locals' might be a legacy of colonialist thinking, where those in a privileged position (academic researchers) impose their power and their language on others. Epistemic violence is defined as 'the harm done to an individual when her understanding of her reality is ignored, obscured, and overridden by another person (or persons) who in words and actions redefine(s) that reality'(178–179). In many cases, people in local contexts might cooperate in these research strategies, as they might copy the language of the academic, privileged researchers. They might exercise a form of agency in acting as researchers, but at the same time the power differences and their own ways of understanding things might stay invisible. Goto critically assesses various methodological approaches, and indicates that the 'challenge is how not to take the proverbial fatal first step of inviting members of faith communities to engage in "theological reflection" as academics call it and know it' (178–179).

Although Goto herself does not speak about children and mainly focuses on oppression in terms of racism, her critical comments might also challenge research on children's spirituality and children's theology. The danger of 'epistemic violence' might also apply to situations of research with children as theologians, although the research with children is often set up as a way to avoid epistemic violence, namely to avoid that children's own voices are not heard and that adults only talk about children, but never listen to them.

It is important to acknowledge the context, and there Goto's argument is in line with Csinos: not all children are the same and it is doing injustice to many children to presume that research about children in a middle-class school in the UK reflects universal truths. However, if research is done in other particular contexts, even by local people, by teachers or catechists who work with children in specific countries in the world, there might be two aspects Goto confronts us with, that are not easy to tackle. First of all, in designing the research, asking questions and analysing it, the academic ways of thinking, the academic theological language might be used and children's own ways of doing and thinking might become invisible due to the dominant way of speaking about children's spirituality or theology. Secondly, because we speak about children, mostly there is also a danger for epistemic injustice because research is done by adults. Children could act as co-researchers, and comment on questionnaires, outcome of data analysis etc. However, this is very intensive and often forgotten.

The discussion about the danger of epistemic injustice helps us to think critically about various aspects of research with children. Are children's own views discussed within the framework of academic concepts, such as 'second naivité'-thinking, for instance (Henckens et al. 2011)? In that case, this might be empowering for children as they are taken seriously and considered as more than not-yet-adults. At the same time, their own 'native' way of thinking and expressing themselves might be overlooked. It might also happen that for the sake of research, children are 'forced into situations or practices which are not common to them in order to start "theologising". Also discussing research results with children might be considered as a way to import a specific jargon to children' (Dillen 2019, 8).

It seems as if Goto's critical analysis leaves us paralysed. Should we stop doing research, as there are so many dangers and as we could harm children, even if we have very good intentions and really want to take them and their particular contexts seriously? That is certainly not what Goto's critical reflection is aimed at. She gives at least three concrete suggestions, to try to avoid epistemic injustice as much as possible, without having the possibility to prevent all forms of harm.

An important first step is reflection about one's own context, privileges and ideas. Goto suggests that it is very important to discuss our own experience as well, and by recognising that the research and specific practices are not 'the only or the right way of coming to understand experiences' (2018, 185).

Secondly, it is important to search for co-researchers. This could be other academics, local leaders, or maybe even children, who might comment on the analysis. In Goto's terms: 'hold back from arbitrating what counts as "theological reflection". The goal would be for co-researchers to *help one another understand* what may be similar and different in their experiences and their ways of making sense of them' (185).

Thirdly, she also suggests to explicitly name power differences or forms of inequality that are present in the process of working together with co-researchers. This could be teachers, or local leaders etc. In this way, awareness about possible shortcomings is shared and recognition is given to the others, due to the complex situation an academic researcher is in. Working on good relations, communication and dialogue is thus very important in all settings, where work with children is done. Goto herself speaks about a 'critical inter-subjective approach to context where researcher(s) and subjects of investigation (often considered co-researchers) practice encountering and negotiating difference as they collaborate in the research process.' She would even call it 'Critical Intersubjectivity' with capitals if privilege and oppression in research are explicitly seen and recognised (189).

Would this be possible in research with children? I will discuss some of the past and ongoing research projects with children, related to my own position as a professor of pastoral and empirical theology at the KU Leuven, Belgium.

4. Children's spirituality in various contexts

I work in a faculty with students from more than 60 countries, but we still have a long way to go to become a decolonial faculty. Nevertheless, I learned a lot from many students and their different contexts and experiences. First, I will broaden our understanding of 'context' and secondly I will discuss one particular research context more in depth, which is a group of children in a slum area in Manila, the Philippines.

4.1. Contexts and their plurality

Understanding the meaning of the term context is not easy. Goto (2018, 85–110) dedicates a whole chapter to this. She distinguishes at least four ways in which the term is used. Context refers to (a) social milieu, (b) a framing device in common speech or specific circumstances, (c) a background story. In these three ways of speaking about context, the 'colloquial use' of context considers it 'as the *background* that allows a theorist to locate or place in the *foreground* the practice, situation or problem under examination' (Goto 2018, 85). It is against this colloquial use of context that Csinos reacts, as he argues that in research on children's spirituality 'context' is only seldomly really a 'locus of concern', as Goto names the fourth way of using the term. Csinos mainly speaks about 'context' in terms of 'social milieu', and thus argues that this singular attention to 'context' is unsatisfactory.

The research projects of my international PhD students have taught me that the social milieu mostly interacts with other aspects. Peter Kantembe for instance studied the spirituality of children in hospitals in Malawi a few years ago (2015). The context of hospitals in Malawi is of course very different from my own context.As Peter Kantembe had worked as a hospital chaplain with children in his own country, he could be considered both as a native and as an academic researcher. His data taught us something about children's spirituality, but also about poverty, the organisation of health care and about local churches and evangelisation in Malawi.

Amy Casteel, an American PhD student, continues her research with adolescents in various countries (Spain, Greece, Belgium) with a specific interest in their migration background. She interviews adolescents who recently arrived in the country and studies how their migration story interrelates with their spirituality. She studies this in various countries and with specific attention for the heterogeneity of the group: she does not want to limit herself to Muslim respondents, as some other researchers in the field of migration do. She also does not want to focus only on so called 'refugees'. She also searches for adolescents with more privileged backgrounds, who go to international schools for example (Casteel and Dillen 2020). She is very aware of the fact that if she would limit herself to one particular context (socio-economic status, migration history, country), she would have to be very cautious to say something 'generic' on children's spirituality in relation to migration. In this way, she tries to avoid one of dangers named by Csinos, namely that the context is sometimes very particular and that some authors make more universal claims based on that specific context. Amy Casteel has a migration background herself, as her own children have, and she will reflect intensely on this own story. Nevertheless, the challenge to try to avoid epistemic injustice by putting children's or adolescent's words in an academic frame, is never totally absent.

Based on the research projects in Leuven, it is clear that aspects of the context as 'social milieu' and as 'a framing device' can and even should go together and can become a more explicit 'locus of concern'.

4.2. Research in the Philippines

I will now focus on one particular context of research, in which I was partly involved myself. In November 2018 a few colleagues and myself visited Saint Vincentian School of Theology (SVST) in Quezon City, which is part of Metro Manila (the National Capital Region) in the Philippines. The dean brought us to the garbage area, called Payatas B, where he serves as a parish priest during the weekends. We visited a specific project within his parish, which is called 'SOW', 'Solidarity with Orphans and Widows'. Since president Duterte started a 'war on drugs', many men were killed, especially those in impoverished areas, due to allegations of drug use or trafficking. Their widows and children have a very difficult life, as they are not only confronted with trauma due to the murder of a loved one, but they are also often blamed and stigmatised by others, and often loose the family income. The parish decided to bring them together for social and spiritual support, and share food together. They have a group for women and one for children.

In 2019 the university gave me the opportunity to set up a research project together with the organisation SOW. Part of the project was also explicitly asking children about their spirituality. We designed the project in the form of 'theological action research' (Cameron et al. 2010) and 'appreciative inquiry' (Cooperrider and Whitney 2005), searching for dreams together, focusing on a bottom up approach. I wanted to prevent that I, as a Belgian scholar, would tell them what to do or to think. I set up the project with the help of a Philippine master student, Karen Papellero, who interviewed the widows earlier, when she was a student at SVST (Papellero 2018). She knew the particular context and the language very well. She spoke with the local leader of the children, a young man who organises activities for them every second Saturday. He organised interviews with the children, based on the questionnaire we designed together with scholars in Leuven and in the Philippines. He was very happy that the research offered him the opportunity to speak with each child individually on his or her spirituality, which was often not possible in the hectic pace of the other activities. The data were transcribed, translated and analysed. We presented the data to the group of children when I visited them in the beginning of December 2019. I asked them whether they wanted to add elements, e.g. on their image of God or on the reason why they pray. Then I asked them which message they would like to give to children in Belgium. At that moment, they had a lot to tell me. In a next step, I told them a *Godly Play* story, and we experienced the story of the 'great family', were 'wondering' together about this story, they were drawing, writing or playing, and then we ate something small together. We concluded that morning with a large meal with the mothers and children and the staff all together. There are many elements of power in this process, even if we tried to work on a basis of mutuality. Most probably, quite a few children wanted to please the native interviewer they knew well, or me, at the moment I visited them. What they said however, is important for this reflection on context – although this article can only shortly deal with the results.

When I asked the children about what children in Belgium should know about them or about God, they told me lots of life lessons, things they have learned that are relevant for them. These are some examples: 'Pray and trust God; Do not go with a stranger if that person look bad; Do not say bad words; Do not forget that God is there; Go to school every day; Finish your study and reach your dreams; Do not be shy to show your talents; Love your parents while they are still there; Do not be rude to other people, especially the poor ones; Do not be shy about God, instead be thankful; Please listen to your parents; Do not be tricked by other people; Eat every day!'

These messages are clearly coloured by their context, in which surviving is very important, and school, food and safety are real concerns for these children. At the same time, God and spirituality do play an important role, as well as the relationships with others and with parents. One cannot say that 'relationality' or 'spirituality' are not important for them. Some people would presume that those children would probably only be occupied by daily struggles. A PhD student from an African country questioned the focus on relationality (see the research of Hay and Nye, mentioned above) in the interpretation of spirituality, while we were discussing research in an international group. He said that he only remembers how he, as a child, was occupied with daily surviving, and referred to the pyramid of needs of Maslow, where food and safety seem to be much more 'basic needs' than 'love and belonging', 'self-esteem' or 'self-actualisation' (Maslow 1943). My own interpretation of the comments of the children in the Philippines, as well as the views of other PhD students, contradicted this presupposition about children's spirituality. The answers of the children on that one question I asked them show they are occupied both with food and with relationality and broader religious aspects. As others have shown as well, a pyramidal presentation of needs does not do justice to the experiences of persons. Nevertheless, both the research itself, and the exchange in an international group, makes me aware about many presuppositions and contextually coloured interpretations.

During the interviews in September 2019, the children also explained how prayer is important for them, and they pray for many things. For safety and for deceased family members, for enough money for daily living and success in school, but they also thank God, trust God and speak about how they feel God's presence in their life. When I explicitly asked in the group whether they also find it difficult to pray, some said yes – although this was not mentioned in the individual interviews. This is only one example of how children co-construct their views related to the particular setting, the questions and the interviewer, as explained by Csinos.

Reflecting on this process of co-construction teaches us something about the process ('how'), and not only the content ('what') of children's spirituality, in line with the findings of Csinos findings. Part of the process of co-construction is the reflection on the personal presuppositions of the researcher (reflexivity). This is also an essential element in an attempt to avoid forms of epistemic injustice, as explained by Goto. However, these presuppositions and the reflection about it might also give rise to epistemic injustice, as the own experiences of the children are framed within the language and the ideas of the researcher.

My presuppositions about God and prayer coloured my questions. I presume spirituality can function as a very important aspect in people's life, but it might also be dangerous when people use spirituality to persuade others how useful it is and to hope spirituality might make their dreams come true. From my liberation theological interest, shared with some colleagues in the Philippines, I am quite critical towards a spirituality that is not combined with social activism and advocacy. So, I explicitly asked a question about certain quotes. Some of the children said in the interview with the Philippine leader: 'I believed in God because … because all of the things He did give to us are trials, and the reason why He took away my father from us is to become strong and to learn how we can stand on our own.'. Someone else said: 'I would like to ask, of all the people why He took my father from us? Why did He give us this kind of curse to my family?'. Another child said: (God loves me) 'because if it's not the will of God, He will not give all of these trials because all of these trials have the right time to end. All of the challenges become right at the end.'. When I discussed my observations about these quotes with colleagues at the university in the Philippines and with the staff of the SOW project, they explained that this is something children sometimes hear from others, but that it does not mean that much. When I met the children, I asked them whether they think it is God who is responsible for the fact that their fathers are killed, or people. This was of course a very direct question. One very vocal child answered 'God'. Then I said: 'yes?'. Then he said: 'no, people'. Others also said: 'no, people are responsible, they have to go to prison'. Later that afternoon, I gave a lecture at a conference for secondary school teachers. One person in the audience asked me something about theologising with children. I referred to this dialogue, a few hours earlier. However, if I refer to this here, I wonder whether I am really doing justice to the children and their context. Although I was trying to take children in their context seriously, I am not sure whether I was really understanding what they wanted to say and what they think. Many elements of power played a role in these conversations and in my analysis.

This article mainly functions as a programmatic and theoretical reflection. Explicit reflection on the role of the context, in its various forms, will have to be done when the different researchers mentioned in this text write extensively about their research results. This is also true for the Philippine context. A few conclusions and suggestions can be drawn now.

5. Conclusion and suggestions

Context is only thematised in a limited way in relation to children's spirituality. The few examples I gave here discuss children's spirituality in a variety of contexts, where not only the regional and socio-economical context matters, but also the particular experiences of a group of children (illness, migration, death of a father, killed in traumatic circumstances). Taking care that research is done by people who know the specific context very well, is possible in many situations. There is however much more that can be done, especially when we want to avoid epistemic injustice in the interpretation of Goto.

When doing research and when writing about research results, it is not only a question of dialogue with local leaders and with researchers from that particular context. It is important to also explicitly name power differences, to search for differences in interpretation and to make sure that the researcher's own interpretations of the children are not overshadowed by views of adults. Making differences visible functions as a very important guideline here. Progress is certainly possible in this regard. The examples of my own research show how complex and difficult it is to try to avoid epistemic injustice.

Reflexivity about one's own context is important. This does not only mean explaining how a researcher comes from a specific context, but also how he or she interprets certain things. I have tried to show a bit of my own struggles and questions in this article.

For further research, it is important to take into account three important 'rules', we can derive from the reflections in this article. First of all: children's spirituality is not static, but is constructed by children in dialogue with others, with parents, teachers, researchers and peers. This means that newer forms of research, maybe also new methodologies, are necessary to make the role of the others much more visible and to shed light on 'how' children's spirituality is co-constructed. Specific study of the context children live in, is therefore very important. Context has a broad meaning: it refers to places where children live (such as schools, families, ...), but also to the socio-cultural context and aspects related to it, such as the gender, age or class of the children at stake. Secondly, research on children's spirituality needs more attention for reflexivity, in order to be more aware of power issues at stake and possible epistemic violence being done to children. Although every research has its shortcomings, this might not prevent researchers to continue their research with children, as the task of learning about their (co-)constructions of spirituality, especially in dialogue with particular contexts, is very important for theology, for practitioners and for children themselves. Who benefits from particular research is, however, always a very important question to ask. Thirdly, this means that, as far as possible, researchers should find ways to include children as co-researchers. In this way we, also students and myself in our Belgian context, can grow. It is my hope that this specific attention for context in its larger meaning, beyond classical views on relations with classmates, schools or parishes, will stimulate other researchers.

Disclosure statement

No potential conflict of interest was reported by the author.

Funding

This work was supported by the KU Leuven, Interfaculty Council for Development Cooperation [ZKD6273].

References

Cameron, H., D. Bhatti, C. Duce, J. Sweeney, and C. Watkins. 2010. *Talking about God in Practice: Theological Action Research and Practical Theology*. London: SCM.

Casteel, A., and A. Dillen. 2020. "Crossing Borders, Changing Faith." In *The Impact of Religion: Migration, Integration and Wellbeing*, edited by M. K. Dahlin, O. Larsson, and A. Winell, 199–212. London: Routledge.

Cooperrider, D., and D. Whitney. 2005. *Appreciative Inquiry. A Positive Revolution in Change*. Oakland: Berrett-Koehler Publishers.

Csinos, D. M. 2018. "From the Ground Up: Cultural Considerations in Research into Children's Spirituality and Theology." *International Journal of Children's Spirituality* 23 (1): 53–66. doi:10.1080/1364436X.2017.1394271.

Csinos, D. M. 2020. *Little Theologians. Children, Culture, and the Making of Theological Meaning*. Kingston: Mcgill-Queen'S University Press.

Dillen, A. 2019. "Research with Children as Theologians: Ethical and Methodological Issues." *HTS Teologiese Studies/Theological Studies* 75 (1): 1–9. doi:10.4102/hts.v75i1.5507.

Goto, C. G. 2018. *Taking on Practical Theology: The Idolization of Context and the Hope for Community*. Vol. 6 of Theology in Practice. Brill: Leiden.

Gruber, J. 2018. *Intercultural Theology: Exploring World Christianity after the Cultural Turn*. Göttingen: Vandenhoeck & Ruprecht.

Hay, D., and R. Nye. 2006. *The Spirit of the Child*. Rev. ed. London: Jessica Kingsley.

Henckens, R., D. Pollefeyt, D. Hutsebaut, A. Dillen, J. Maex, and E. De Boeck. 2011. *Geloof in Kinderen? Levensbeschouwelijke Groei Bij Kinderen in Kaart Gebracht: Opzet, Methode En Resultaten Van Empirisch Onderzoek Bij Leerkrachten Rooms-katholieke Godsdienst En Hun Leerlingen in De Derde Graad Lager Onderwijs En De Eerste Graad Secundair Onderwijs [Faith in Children? Childrens Religious Growth Mapped: Goal, Method and Results of Empirical Research on Teachers in Roman Catholic Religion and Their Pupils in Third and Seventh Grade]*. Leuven: Peeters, Instrumenta Theologica.

Kantembe, P. C. 2015. "Nurturing Children's Spirituality in Hospitals: Childhood Studies and Their Theological Implications for Child-centered Pastoral Care in Hospitals in Malawi." PhD diss., KU Leuven.

Knibbe, K., and H. Kupari. 2020. "Theorizing Lived Religion: Introduction." *Journal of Contemporary Religion* 35 (2): 157–176. doi:10.1080/13537903.2020.1759897.

Kummer, A. M. 2019. *Men, Spirituality and Gender-Specific Biblical Hermeneutics*. Leuven: Peeters.

Maslow, A. 1943. "A Theory of Human Motivation." *Psychological Review* 50: 370–396. doi:10.1037/h0054346.

Mercer, J. A., D. L. Matthews, and S. Walz. 2004. "Children in Congregations: Congregations as Context for Children's Spiritual Growth. Chap. 16." In *Children's Spirituality: Christian Perspectives, Research, and Applications*, edited by K. E. Lawson and S. May. 2nd ed, 249–265. Eugene, OR: Cascade.

Mercer, J. A. 2005. *Welcoming Children: A Practical Theology of Childhood*. St. Louis, MO: Chalice Press.

Mercer, J. A. 2008. *Girl Talk, God Talk: Why Faith Matters to Adolescent Girls and Their Parents*. San Francisco: Jossey Bass.

Papellero, Ma. Karen. 2018. "We Will Live: Hope and Vision among Surviving Families of Extrajudicial Killings" (unpublished Master thesis in Theology, Saint Vincent School of Theology, Adamson University, Manila), 2018.

Pollefeyt, D., and J. Bouwens. 2014. *Identity in Dialogue: Assessing and Enhancing Catholic School Identity: Research Methodology and Research Results in Catholic Schools in Victoria, Australia*. Zürich: LIT Verlag.

Riegel, U., and K. Kindermann. 2016. "The Impact of Participatory Learning on Attitude: A Quasi-Experimental Study in German Primary Schools." *Journal of Empirical Theology* 29 (1): 1–23. doi:10.1163/15709256-12341334.

Schweitzer, F., and R. Boschki, eds. 2018. *Researching Religious Education: Classroom Processes and Outcomes*. Vols. 12 of Glaube–Wertebildung–Interreligiosität: Berufsorientierte Religionspädagogik. Münster: Waxmann Verlag.

Spivak, G. 1988. "Can the Subaltern Speak?" In *Marxism and the Interpretation of Culture*, edited by L. Grossberg and C. Nelson, 66–111. Houndmills: Macmillan.

Wollrad, E. 2005. *Weissein Im Widerspruch: Feministische Perspektiven Auf Rassismus, Kultur Und Religion [Whiteness in Opposition: Feminist Perspectives on Racism, Culture and Religion]*. Königstein: Ulrike Helmer Verlag.

An inclusive spiritual education

Joyce E. Bellous

ABSTRACT
I define human spirituality as a sense of felt connection, which is central to a human capacity to survive and thrive. That is, the spiritual lies at the foundation of human experience, so that everyone is spiritual, and typically, people use religious language to express spiritual concerns. In this paper, I lay out an inclusive approach to spiritual education that gets beneath religious and spiritual tensions to focus on human need. In offering the approach, and perhaps an attitude to the humanity of our learners, this essay describes four spiritual styles. Each one relies on a specific currency. The four currencies are, namely, word, emotion, symbol and action. I unpack the styles to show how, taken together, they create a holistic and humane literacy curriculum that welcomes children and youth into classroom experiences despite their personal religious differences or, perhaps, the indifference they bring with them to class.

Introduction

As part of my research into human spirituality, which extends over more than 20 years, I came to define human spirituality as a sense of felt connection. I first published this view in *Educating Faith* (Bellous [2006] 2015). That research grew out of involvement with an international group of religious educators who taught in what North Americans call public school. The group included Catholics, Protestants, Jews, Buddhists, adherents to what was called New Age thought, as well as many who were atheists and agnostics.

The primary reason for its diversity was that, in many countries, religion is a required subject. As examples, colleagues from Scandinavian countries and The Netherlands taught religion but identified personally as having no faith in the existence of God, or as believing that it's impossible to know whether God exists.

In this research environment, my attention was drawn to the human side of spirituality – the human spirit – that I defined as an agent of relational communication based on a sense[1] of felt connection (Gendlin 1962, 1981) – that is, spirituality is a human capacity for connection. *Educating Faith* describes spiritual work as the making of meaning, constructed out of the ordinary experience through five existential processes that typify childhood, i.e., sociological, neurological, cultural, biological and psychological processes. (Bellous [2006] 2015, 9) Due to our diversity, it was important to form a view of spirituality, and an educational approach to it, that was inclusive of the differences that typified our group.

It's compelling to consider how the topic of human spirituality has advanced scientifically in the last 20 years, e.g., from the discovery of mirror neurons in 1994, which my colleagues and I knew nothing about, to research on the *Vagus Nerve Complex* that sustains connections within the body if and when people flourish in relationally healthy settings, or that stores enormous, persistent harm under unhealthy conditions that produce trauma. (van der Kolk 2015) In the last 20 years, scientific development of spirituality got another boost from American psychologist Lisa Miller. She researches psychology and spirituality. Her book, *The Spiritual Child* (2015), recounts work that, in her view, has established children's spirituality as a scientific fact. She also edited *The Oxford Handbook of Psychology and Spirituality* (2012).

My purpose in this essay is to say that the human need for a sense of felt connection is best developed through an inclusive spiritual education. This is an education that allows children and adolescents to develop maturity by recognising their tendency to use one or more of four spiritual currencies, namely, word, emotion, symbol or action. The assumption here is that spiritual work is grounded on our ability and willingness to make meaningful connections with others, and under favourable conditions, to do so in a way that improves a situation or makes the world a better place.

In terms of spiritual education, as a formative level of learning, children and youth are encouraged to develop and comprehend these four Spiritual Styles. In this approach, spiritual neglect is understood to impoverish children and youth. Spiritual poverty expresses itself in dangerous activities taken up during adolescence. More positively, the opportunity to enjoy a spiritually rich setting, in which children and youth feel included, provides the young with resources to individuate themselves and also to become effective members of healthy communities. A second assertion is linked to the first: in an inclusive spiritual education, there is no room for denigrating or dismissing religion and religious language.

In order to make the case, I first look at the relationship between religion and spirituality from the perspectives of educational and psychological research. After that, I describe the four Spiritual Styles named above and outline four types of literacy that develop them. The four styles and four types of literacy form an inclusive spiritual education that provides a secure base for human flourishing. My aim in providing the four types of literacy is to encourage faith educators to develop the fullest sense of humanity and spirituality in their learners.

Spirituality and religion

In *Educating Faith* I distinguish spirituality and religion by saying that spirituality lives in a space that opens up between the personal and material, between an objective and subjective experience (Bellous [2006] 2015). The human spirit is an agent of and repository for accumulated meaning that is derived from exposure to experience. As a human capacity, spirituality is a relation that builds meaning based on the five existential processes named above (sociology, neurology, culture, biology and psychology). The psychological aspect of object relating unifies the other four by organising them into a worldview, or lens for looking at the world. (Bellous [2006] 2015, 26)[2]

The meaning one makes acts back on experience to establish and perpetuate assumptions, beliefs and values that form that worldview. By 11 or 12 years old, every child has a worldview based on experience. That worldview acts back on how a child or adolescent interprets life and establishes what she or he believes can be expected from it.

Yet spirituality is an ambiguous term. Some think of it as a basic human capacity; others think of it as a way of life, e.g., a Christian, Buddhist or an atheistic way of life.[3] Both ways of thinking about spirituality are useful, but spirituality, whether the capacity or way of life, is healthy only as long as the following spiritual needs are met:

> Every human being has a spiritual need to celebrate, mark significant moments, bear witness to truths learned about life, play, tell their story, grieve, mourn, lament, connect with the past, make significant journeys, express themselves symbolically, seek purpose and meaning, ask ultimate questions, have a satisfactory way to think and speak about the beginning and end of life, survive, flourish, experience longing and enjoy its satisfaction, relax, cope with life circumstances, be seen, be heard, have a name that is remembered, be part of a larger community, organize experience meaningfully so as to make sense of it, maintain human dignity and see the future as hopeful. (Bellous [2006] 2015, 19)

To say that spirituality is a human capacity is also to say that spirituality is more than religion and to posit that everyone is spiritual, whether or not they are religious. American psychologist Lisa Miller goes further. In *The Spiritual Child* (2015, 6–7]) she argues, using scientific data, that spirituality is 'an inner sense of living relationship to a higher power (God, nature, spirit, universe, the creator, or whatever your word is for the ultimate loving, guiding life-force).'

In making this assertion, she implies that spirituality involves two parties: there is someone who has a capacity for felt connection with the Unseen and there is *Something There* (Hay 2006) that acts back through that connection to provide relational meaning and support. This particular point is logical but not necessarily credible to everyone. If it were both logical and universally credible, there would be few people who believe that God (or something like God) does not exist and few who think it is impossible to know whether God exists. Yet we all know perfectly reasonable people who hold both of these views. At this point, it's important to say that, even in the face of the scientific support for Miller's views, Canadian cultural history and values are best served by including, respecting and supporting religious and secular, theistic and atheistic/agnostic worldviews.

A central aspect of Miller's view is that this 'living relationship' must be personal and personally sought, secured and lived out in the daily exercise of one's values and behaviour because the connection builds what she calls an inner spiritual compass. In her view, this compass is an innate, concrete faculty. Like emotional intelligence, it is part of our biological endowment. She asserts that it can be cultivated. I would add that, without the civility identified in the previous paragraph, i.e., intentional and respectful inclusion of difference, this compass might be thrown off kilter if spirituality, religion, atheism, agnosticism, or secularism are so thoroughly disdained within a social environment, that the compass is rendered *almost* useless.

Miller notes that her evidence for an inner compass is 'hard, indisputable, and rigorously scientific.' (Miller 2015, 6) Is she making a case for the necessity of religion? The question is complex. Miller cites a twin study carried out by Kenneth Kendler that asked about the relationship between spirituality and religion. He concluded that, in his research with nearly 2000 adult twins, it was shown statistically that 'in people's lived experience, personal spirituality is a different concept from adherence to religion or choice of religious denomination.' (Miller 2015, 7)

However, there is not clear evidence that religion and spirituality are unrelated. The quality of the spiritual experience was shown to be 'a sense of close personal relationship' to God (et cetera) and a vital source of daily guidance. (2015, 7) Miller also notes that in Kendler's research 'spirituality did not meaningfully correlate with one specific religious denomination [or tradition]; ... [because] there are highly spiritual people who [do not] adhere to any specific religious denomination [or tradition].' (Miller 2015, 8)

Yet the complexity of her scientific investigations has other important features. Miller made use of a 1997 study, a landmark scientific article published in the *American Journal of Psychiatry* that provided evidence of a hugely beneficial dimension of spirituality that was empirically derived. The study uncovered the significance of 'a personal relationship with the transcendent' and argued that the relationship makes a crucial and valuable contribution to 'good health, mental well-being, fulfillment and success.' (Miller 2015, 7–8) What, then, are the implications for religion and spirituality? Are religion and spirituality necessarily linked?

Miller provides a caveat. She notes empirical research that methodically identified what is *not* meant by personal spirituality. In this data, spirituality is unrelated statistically to strict adherence to a religion or a creed without a sense of personal choice or ownership. She goes further to say that 'rigid adherence to a creed without a sacred personal relationship is very different from [what she calls] natural spirituality and is often associated with dangerous risk-taking, including unprotected, high-risk, and abusive sexual activity.' (2015, 8) She observes further that, while personal devotion is highly protective against heavy substance use and abuse, rigid adherence to a creed without a sense of the sacred relationship does not prevent against substance abuse. (2015, 8) From my perspective, the core definition of human spirituality as a sense of felt connection or a felt sense of connection is shown to support her assertions about the mismatch between religion and spirituality, under the unfavourable conditions that she describes.

In summary, religion and spirituality are significantly related under the condition that religious creeds and practices support personal devotion and the freedom that's implied when a tradition is taken on willingly and authentically. Further, to disdain religion is, in my view, uncivil because people most often use religious language to convey spirituality. But if spirituality is defined as a felt sense of connection (to which Miller adds the Divine, a Higher Power, the Universe or an Ideal relation), the absence of a felt sense of connection within religious settings does nothing to enhance the spiritual dimension of human life, as her research on risk-taking behaviour confirms.

So what to say about religion and spirituality – a complex question fraught with difficulty? It's clear to me that bad religion hurts people. Religious harm may render useless the spiritual capacities of human life. Yet one question stands out. If human spiritual needs are met, would we have a bad religion?

In terms of meeting spiritual needs, children are different than grown-ups. While they eventually will choose what to put faith in personally, when they're young, they need to be situated within a narrative that's larger than their own small lives so they can make sense of the world and locate their place within it. They need a conceptual, emotional, symbolic, action-oriented foundation on which to build belief. Sigmund Freud was disastrously wrong in his passionately held view that children should be without religious education so they could eventually choose faith for themselves – or not choose it. He was wrong about how faith works and wrong about how spiritual needs develop in human beings. (Rizzuto 1998)

If adults choose to be non-religious, it behoves them to offer children narratives to meet spiritual needs that arise in them naturally. These narratives allow children to live in peace (without anxiety) until they make workable narratives for themselves. A maturing soul, as Pascal would say, moves from simple ignorance, through inquiry, to wise ignorance, or as Paul Ricoeur put it, from naiveté through critical reflection to the second naiveté. But simple ignorance and naiveté require an education. That education must be a foundation on which the young can build an authentic life and acquire the knowledge and skills to become well integrated with others.

Spiritually rich environments

How might an inclusive spiritual education provide the means for developing an authentic and a well-integrated self? Spiritual work weaves a web of meaning that supports personal and communal dimensions of human life. Spiritual work offers the young a basis for positive, hopeful expectations regarding their ability to be authentic as well as communal selves.

The developed capacity to be both authentic and well-integrated is a primary goal for a mature life. Spiritual work wraps itself around a willingness and ability to name ourselves authentically and situate that identity within a community of people who matter to us – to whom we are committed. At the heart of this work are skills of recruitment – of being able to secure appropriate attention for oneself, and at the same time show interest in others. (Derber 2000) Spiritual work is the foundation of civility in which we realise we are unique, but the difference is not allowed to create distance and separation (not to mention arrogance) from others who also wish to be free to be themselves while in community with others.

In terms of the development of a fully orbed self, this understanding of authenticity is not built on the basis of solitary confinement characteristic of individualism that dominated United States cultures from the mid-twentieth century onwards and was an extreme form historically. Spiritual work finds a way to be authentic and communal. This may not be easy, but is it possible in the twenty-first century? And what sort of educational practices help ground its possibility?

One opportunity opens up as we assess our spiritual styles and realise the ways that people are similar to and different from each other. The following description of Spiritual Styles conveys the way people try to improve a situation or make the world a better place. Understanding these styles help interpret the good intentions of others, even if they seem to be speaking a different language. The following section outlines four Spiritual Styles and the currency inherent in each.[4]

Before describing the styles, it is fair to ask what motivates an inclusive spiritual education. In order to create a healthy learning environment, teachers actively attend to the greatest inequalities in the classroom, which are based on unequal distributions of attention. That inequality results in an inability for some children to recruit the interest of others in them. Because recruiting is a social skill, children may need help as they try to get others to be interested in them. If their failure becomes chronic, they may learn to be irritating due to perpetual disappointment, or learn to disappear as a way to relieve that disappointment. Those who do not fit into a setting cannot secure the positive attention that would allow them to relax when they are with others. A lack of skill in recruiting attention is a powerful determinant of future thriving.

One way to include everyone is to provide a style rich environment. Children whose spiritual style differs from the dominant ethos may be marginalised, ignored and seen as difficult or uninteresting. In the section that follows, I describe Spiritual

Styles by using a case study for each one. A Spiritual Styles Assessment was developed in 2009. There is an adult version and a children's version. While administering the Assessment over the last decade, it has become apparent that adults most often see a profound connection between the style they use as adults and the way they were as children. For that reason, the styles are described using scenarios from childhood. Each style description includes aspects of an educational thought experiment for an inclusive spiritual education that is developed from my classroom experience over the last decade.

Childhood example: Nora – word

Nora's friends do not understand why she would rather attend a debate than go to the shopping centre with friends. She is part of the debate club at school and loves to hear two sides arguing over the meaning of a word. She loves to win. Much of her time is spent with her nose in a book. She wants to know the precise meaning of words. She was angry in science class the other day when she asked her teacher about the meaning of a word. She thought the teacher's answer was inadequate because it left out a lot. Nora defends her ideas at dinner. She corrects her brother, sister and parents if they are not being clear. Nora's dad gets frustrated because she asks for reasons when he asks her to do something, rather than just doing what she is asked. When she makes a decision, she likes to tell people why, even if no one stays around to listen. She loves to write and hopes to be an author.

Word style users

Education Goal: To converse with the philosopher in order to develop **Cognitive Literacy** by teaching learners to become reasonable people and by helping them to practice

- Using words and reason to establish conceptual relationships
- Coming to see what they think and asking themselves if they want to continue to think in this way
- Using precision, accuracy and conceptual clarity
- Analysing, comparing, contrasting, asking and responding to good questions

Childhood example: Sara – emotion

Sara loves her school. It is a performing Arts school and she is involved in the school's production of Wind in the Willows. She feels a sense of belonging when she is with her friends singing and dancing on stage. Her friends love her and are drawn to her warm, infectious laugh but sometimes they are not sure that she still likes them. Teachers praise her beautiful voice and her ability to light up the stage. Sara often makes decisions based on how she feels. Sometimes this works out well. Other times, her choices leave her with regret. She comes home from school every day flying high on her interactions with others. Even though she spends time telling her mom about her relationships, she also complains that she does not have anyone who feels really close to her. She has a hard time completing her homework. She calls friends on the phone or texts when she said she would do her work and often feels unmotivated. Sara knows that something is important in her life if she is moved to tears or something makes her so excited she feels like dancing. Her goal is to make people happy.

Emotion style users

Educational Goal: To sing with the Dancer in order to develop **Emotional Literacy** by achieving self-awareness and self-management (self-regulation) and to practice

- Emotional awareness and self-regulation
- Clarity of emotional expression through the following activities:
- Movement – Feeling
- Acting
- Learning through the Arts, music and experience

Childhood example: Alex – symbol

Alex attends a private elementary school known for its high academic standards. He recently told his parents that he believes he does not fit in. In his opinion, teachers at his school over teach; they tell the children what to think. 'They have no imagination,' he told his parents. 'I can't be creative. I prefer to learn by exploring mysteries, rather than reading text books.' He loves stories about the Bermuda Triangle and Stonehenge. These places are mysterious and allow him to wonder. His teachers tell Alex about the certainties of science and mathematics, but he cannot help wondering about what seems like strange aspects of life and the world around him. He often feels frustrated with the pace of his school day and wishes there was more time to think about things. He believes there must be more to life than what he sees. As he sits quietly on the bank of the river across from his home, he sees the wind blowing through the trees and hears water rushing by him. In this place, Alex feels at peace with the world and close to God.

Symbol style users

Educational Goal: To respond with the Mystic in order to develop **Imaginative Literacy** and to practice

- Enjoying Quietness
- Thinking Imaginatively
- Practising Stillness
- Enjoying Beauty
- Participating in Ritual and Symbol
- Learning through meditation, from Nature and by careful observation

Childhood example: Mark – action

When Mark was 4-years old, he discovered that some people in the world do not have clean water. He was surprised and knew it was not fair. How could we have so much clean water in Canada when other people did not have any? He knew he could do something to help. When he was 5-years old, he started to raise money to build a well in Africa. The whole idea of helping people in Africa got started when he built a little well in kindergarten while he was doing a science project about pulleys and levers. He got the idea to start collecting money for a real well in the little well he built. Mark decided to ask his friends to help and some did. He told his teacher he was frustrated with kids in his class who did not want to participate. He was passionate about the cause and wanted to build three wells, three sets of latrines and three hand washing stations. He wanted to tell kids in Africa about clean water so they would be safe. When anyone asks Mark why he does it, he says, 'This is my passion, this is what makes me feel good.'

Action style users

Educational Goal: To accompany the Change Agent in order to develop **Social Literacy** by achieving social awareness and relational management in order to learn how to maintain a healthy relational environment and to practice

- Involvement in the world with those who are marginalised or in poverty
- Acting for Justice
- Personal engagement in change
- Perceiving patterns in human interaction that create injustice
- Seeing what's there, what's not there and what could be there
- Learning by doing, observing and being with others who are working for Justice

Four types of literacy

Given the four styles and the currency, each one relies upon as people work for good and work together (word, emotion, symbol and action), the following four types of literacy are central to a healthy, holistic, spiritual education. In what follows, I outline a plausible approach for developing these four types of literacy. The ideas that are included are based on classroom work I have carried out over the last decade. This section is also an invitation for readers to join in the project of creating an inclusive spiritual education.

Cognitive Literacy: A fully developed willingness and ability to think about the meaning of words, concepts, sentences, ideas and their inter-relatedness, until a sense of clarity is achieved.

Skills:

- Develop clarity and clear thinking
- Use reason, which is a stubbornly persistent effort to get clear about something. (Gottlieb 2016, xi).
- Develop conversational skills, e.g., Socratic conversation and Aristotelian deliberation.
- Play with the meaning of words and ask questions, as some examples:
    - How do the concepts form?
    - How do conceptual analysis and informal logic work?
    - How do words work in relation to other words?
    - What does coherence look like and what practices help to build clarity?

Emotional Literacy: A fully developed willingness and ability to gain self-awareness and develop self-regulation, as well as accurately reading others in a way they can affirm.

Skills:

- Develop Self-Awareness
- Achieve Self-Regulation
    - Reflection on self-consciousness: Thought recognition
    - Thought stopping and thought managing
    - Learning from what's happening in one's own heart
    - Bring one's own meaning to bear on one's own action.
    - Recognise and acknowledge the meaning others make.

Imaginative Literacy: A fully developed penetrating perception of whole and partial worlds, whether visible or beyond ordinary seeing; a developed ability to make sense of other people, entities, narratives and events that are (ultimately) meaningfully communicated in various ways, (e.g., in poetry, novels).

Skills:

- Develop moral/aesthetic/social abilities to see what's going on
- Achieve a responsive capacity for empathy and mindfulness
    - Spiritual disciplines and facilitating rituals

- Rituals built into worship and everyday life
- Quiet wondering
- Experiences of other whole worlds, e.g., in literature, sacred texts

Social Literacy: A fully developed willingness and ability to be authentic – to be oneself in all places, times and events at the same time that one is well integrated with others who matter – whether they are similar to or different from oneself.

Skills:

- Develop an authentic voice
- Achieve integrative skills that allow one to remain oneself while with others
  - Social Awareness based on deep self and other understanding
  - Social Facility: skills that enhance social interaction
  - Reflection on practice
  - A sense of social justice and responses to individual issues that arise
  - Perceiving systemic injustice and responding to ameliorate it

Conclusion

The four scenarios and types of literacy form an inclusive spiritual education. As they work towards what they consider to be improvements, Nora, Sara, Alex and Mark use different currencies to make their contributions. Teachers, parents and adults serve learners' needs by recognising and understanding the roles that their spiritual strategies are trying to accomplish. In an inclusive setting, spiritual needs are recognised and met, whether a teacher is focused on spirituality as a human capacity or as a way of life. Since the human spirit is an agent of human flourishing, we are well-advised to ensure that we understand the languages children use as they attempt to make the world a better place and find a secure place within it.

Notes

1. I treat the two expressions 'a sense of felt connection' and 'a felt sense of connection' as similar experientially, although I don't claim that the terms are identical.
2. Spirituality is a mid-point reality between subjective and objective realities; e.g., what Martin Buber calls a relation that he thought of as a spiritual connection. As he put it, 'In the beginning is the relation – as a category of being, as readiness, as a form that reaches out to be filled . . . .' He identified a spiritual link between self and object by using childhood as an actual and metaphorical ground for describing subject/object relations, i.e., for his own theory of object relating, although he didn't use that term.
3. Some would use the word religion here but I think we need a broader expression so I chose the way of life.

4. Spiritual Styles Assessments, in adult and children's versions, are available by contacting tallpinepress@gmail.com Bellous' initial work on spiritual styles was based on Corinne Ware's book, Discover Your Spiritual Type, An Alban Institute Publication, 1995, 1997, 200). The styles were worked out in *Educating Faith* (Bellous [2006] 2015) and in Joyce E. Bellous and Dan Sheffield *Conversations that Change Us (2007; 2017).* Spiritual Styles were used by David Csinos in his Master thesis at McMaster Divinity and in David M. Csinos, *Children's Ministry that fits, Wipf and Stock, 2011.*

Disclosure statement

No potential conflict of interest was reported by the author.

References

Bellous, J. E. [2006] 2015. *Educating Faith: An Approach to Christian Spiritual Formation*. Toronto: Clements.

Derber, C. 2000. *The Pursuit of Attention*. New York: Oxford University Press.

Gendlin, E. 1962. *Focusing*. New York: Bantam.

Gendlin, E. 1981. *Experiencing and the Creation of Meaning*. New York: Free Press of Glencoe.

Gottlieb, A. 2016. *The Dream of Reason*. New York: W.W. Norton and Company.

Hay, D. 2006. *Something There*. West Conshohocken: Temple Foundation Press.

Miller, L., ed. 2012. *The Oxford Handbook of Psychology and Spirituality*. New York: Oxford University Press.

Miller, L. 2015. *The Spiritual Child*. New York: St Martin's Press.

Rizzuto, A.-M. 1998. *Why Did Freud Reject God?* New Haven: Yale University Press.

van der Kolk, B. 2015. *The Body Keeps the Score: Brain, Mind and Body in the Healing of Trauma*. New York: Penguin Books.

Index

Note: **Bold** page numbers refer to tables; *italic* page numbers refer to figures and page numbers followed by "n" denote endnotes.